You Were
Never Meant
to Do It All

You Were Never Meant to Do It All

A *40-Day Devotional*
on the Goodness of Being Human

KELLY M. KAPIC

BrazosPress
a division of Baker Publishing Group
Grand Rapids, Michigan

© 2025 by Kelly M. Kapic

Published by Brazos Press
a division of Baker Publishing Group
Grand Rapids, Michigan
BrazosPress.com

Printed in the United States of America

Library of Congress Cataloging-in-Publication Data
Names: Kapic, Kelly M., 1972– author.
Title: You were never meant to do it all : a 40-day devotional on the goodness of being human / Kelly M. Kapic.
Description: Grand Rapids, Michigan : Brazos Press, a division of Baker Publishing Group, [2025]
Identifiers: LCCN 2024045346 | ISBN 9781540968982 (cloth) | ISBN 9781493450282 (ebook)
Subjects: LCSH: Devotional exercises. | Christian life.
Classification: LCC BV4832.3 .K37 2025 | DDC 242—dc23/eng/20241122
LC record available at https://lccn.loc.gov/2024045346

Stories told in this book reflect the author's present recollections of experiences over time. Some names and characteristics have been changed, some events have been compressed, and some dialogue has been re-created.

Cover design by Studio Gearbox, David Carlson

Baker Publishing Group publications use paper produced from sustainable forestry practices and postconsumer waste whenever possible.

25 26 27 28 29 30 31   7 6 5 4 3 2 1

To Margot

My beloved daughter,
your brilliant mind is matched only
by the depth of your compassion
and your strength by your tenderness.
Your smile, zeal for life, and generous loving spirit
illuminate the world around you.
I am so grateful to call you my daughter.

Contents

A Question and an Invitation

What does God expect from you? In a day, a week, a lifetime? Even when we don't explicitly ask that question, our intuitions about it contain such a presence and power over us that we will do well to investigate it more closely. The last thing we want is to be driven by irrational and unhealthy impulses that we have somehow confused with God's will.

Answering this question is often far more difficult than assumed, partly because it can be hard to distinguish between God's opinion on these matters and the opinions of parents, employers, and countless others shaping our cultural moment. For various historical, social, and economic reasons, the values of speed and industry shape the answers for many of us. Productivity and efficiency often turn out to be our highest and most formative values. As we will see later in this devotional, while there is good in these values, they are certainly not God's highest values.

For many of us, the voices in our heads and hearts are always demanding more: more productivity at work, more time with the kids, more exercise, more prayer, more money, more church involvement, more social engagement, more quiet time, more sleep, more home improvement—more, more, more. And amid the onslaught of needs and demands, we often just feel like we're letting everyone down. That is partly because we imagine that we can always do more. But maybe we need to retrain these internal voices. After all, they often don't speak for God!

Another reason answering the question of what God expects from us is tricky is that we struggle to understand how God's grace and our actions relate. On the one hand, we face the very real danger of subtle forms of legalism—in which our actions make us acceptable to God, as if his love for us were contingent on our behavior. That kind of attitude turns our relationship with God into a series of transactions, which tends to breed exhaustion, bitterness, anger, and self-loathing. In a culture that highly prizes productivity and efficiency, God begins to look more like an unrelenting boss than a compassionate and knowing Father. If you regularly experience these symptoms, you should probably talk this through with a trusted Christian friend, mentor, pastor, or counselor. Living on edge before God does not need to be your ongoing experience.

That said, I have often seen an overcorrection from the other side. Legitimately worried about the threat of legalism, we become tempted to speak of grace in such a way that personal agency, vocation, effort, and wisdom are undermined. It saddens me how often I have heard well-meaning leaders avoid a potential lapse into legalism by undercutting legitimate discipleship. It may sound strange, but people making this mistake often treat expressions of determination, self-control, and community-oriented decisions as signs of idolatry rather than God-honoring attempts at faithfulness. Can't we avoid legalism on the one hand and passive paralysis on the other?

We are indeed secure with God: we can rest in the love of the Father, the grace of the Son, and the abiding fellowship of the Spirit. We are saved by grace, kept by grace, and never graduate from grace. Amen and amen. Nevertheless, honestly acknowledging the problem of sin and the wonder of grace does not undermine the goodness of our creator God and the good creation he designed. Grace does not devalue our bodies or downplay our faculties (e.g., our mind, will, and affections); rather, it establishes their importance and effectiveness. As we will see, the Creator is the same God as the Redeemer.

Consequently, to better appreciate God's "expectations for us," we would do well to examine the goodness of how God has made us. In this devotional, we will pay particular attention to the most neglected aspect of our *good* creaturely existence— our appropriate limits. Acknowledging our creaturely limits does not set rest and effort against one another but coordinates them in terms of God's wise design.

God has not designed us to do everything, be everywhere, or know everything. We can value our work, our bodies, and our relationships without thinking we must have endless energy, always be strong, or have unending emotional reserves. God simply didn't create us in this way. Thus, we must stop pretending we are infinite (without limits), learning instead to be faithful within our finitude (i.e., creaturely limits). Within those limits, our agency is honored but not deified. Here wisdom guides our various vocations, helping us navigate giving and receiving, exertion and respite, life and love. Living in this dynamic is an opportunity for faithfulness rather than a burden to be crushed by.

The vision I hope you get through these brief devotional entries is one of a truly humane and godly Christian life. What do you expect of yourself? Of others? What does God expect of you? Maybe it's time to slow down and take forty days to wrestle with these questions. Along the way, we will explore the value of our bodies, of our communities, and of process. We will begin to see beauty in humility, dependence, and rest. My great hope and prayer is that through this process you will not only see afresh the wonder and goodness of God but also feel more secure in his wisdom and love. From this position of security, you can freely love and serve others, even while avoiding a messianic complex, unhealthy misunderstandings, or misapplications of the gospel.

This devotional is based on the book *You're Only Human*, and interested readers are encouraged to read that book for fuller explanations and applications of the various ideas I can only hint at here. With its distinct format and style, this volume is intended as a jumping-off point for meditation. Each entry is 850 words or less, and each is followed by relevant questions that can be used for personal or small group reflection.

This book primarily exists because I heard from busy business folks, prison chaplains, pastors, and small group leaders who regularly wrote or called to say, "I love *You're Only Human*, but people I want to share it with find it too long or too intimidating. Can you give us a shorter version?" What you hold in your hands is my earnest attempt to answer that request as faithfully as possible. There are about three or four devotional entries for each of the ten chapters in *You're Only Human*. Finally, this devotional emphasizes slow reading and pastorally relevant questions, and my hope and prayer is that this book might be read with great benefit by God's people.

Facing Our Limits

The result of busyness is that an individual is very seldom permitted to form a heart.

—Søren Kierkegaard, journal entry

All of us bounce between the illusion that we are in control and the world's demonstration that we are not. When the brokenness of the world hits our human limitations, it often strains our emotions, will, and understanding. Whether through tragedy or the natural process of aging, we are all repeatedly reminded that life is fragile and that we are limited creatures, dependent on God and one another. Such reminders might come by way of a coworker who has greater intellectual gifts, or a fellow athlete who is faster, or an aging parent whose waning emotional and psychological stability threatens the health of our relationship with them. As we live in these tensions, we start to sense that we have far less control of the world and even of ourselves than we once imagined. Some people respond to these tensions by living as passive victims, whereas others aggressively try to seize as much control as possible. Many of us bounce between these two extremes.

Slowness . . . nurtures attention, and speed shatters it.

—Johann Hari, *Stolen Focus: Why You Can't
Pay Attention—and How to Think Deeply Again*
(New York: Random House, 2022), 36.

Despite our limits, many of us live as though the weight of the world and all its responsibilities are on our own shoulders. And it exhausts us. Behind the patient smiles on our faces we hide a weariness or even a lingering rage toward the endless demands on us, our unrealized dreams, and the relationships that don't seem to work well anymore.

The odd thing is that even when we run into our inevitable limits, we often hang on to the delusion that if we just work harder, squeeze tighter, and become more efficient, we can eventually regain control. We imagine we can keep our children safe, our incomes secure, and our bodies whole. But denying our creaturely limits cripples us in ways we probably don't realize. It distorts our view of God, ourselves, and Christian spirituality.

How do we handle the fact that others are often brighter, stronger, and more attractive than we are? How are you navigating this aspect of life? As you try to keep up, are you regularly exhausted and constantly strung out? Do you experience a consistent feeling of guilt about how little you accomplish each day? Are you weighed down by a sense of how much needs to get done and how little progress you are making? How are you feeling about your plans, hopes, and dreams as you have grown in your awareness of your own weaknesses?

At my work, there are always people and projects that need more attention than I can give. Others face similar frustrations: the warehouse operator can always become more efficient with inventory; the real estate agent has never sold enough houses; the stay-at-home parent never seems to get to that neglected mess in the kids' closet. Counselors might have asked better questions; teachers could be better prepared for classes; and students wish they could focus longer. We all constantly collide with our limits. Your work circumstances probably differ from mine, but if you are like me, you often end your day wondering whether you have done "enough."

This feeling of never having done enough affects not just our employment but every area of our lives. We talk about how we should exercise more, be more involved with our churches, further develop our minds, or invest more in our families and communities. We have so many opportunities to explore and so many needs to meet! We continually sense our shortcomings, our longings to be more and to do more, and yet we often run smack dab into our physical and emotional limits. So how should we respond to the endless needs and demands—and our guilt at being unable to meet them?

When have we done enough?

Here we face a crucial question: Are we *required* to overcome these perceived shortcomings? Some people treat these limitations as *always* indicating a moral deficiency of some kind or as

It is in ordinary life that our stories unfold, tales of conceiving, bearing and giving birth, of trial and death and rising to new life out of the ashes of the old. . . . Christianity is inescapably down-to-earth and incarnational—I say 'inescapably,' as most of us, at one time or another, try to avoid the implications of an incarnational faith. The Christian religion asks us to place our trust not in ideas, and certainly not in ideologies, but in a God who was vulnerable enough to become human and die, and who desires to be present to us in our everyday circumstances. And because we are human, it is in the realm of the daily and the mundane that we must find our way to God.

—Kathleen Norris, *The Quotidian Mysteries: Laundry, Liturgy and "Women's Work"* (New York: Paulist Press, 1998), 77–78.

an obstacle in a competition that can and should be conquered. But is that approach true to reality?

One common response in the West is to seek self-improvement through better training and organization. We skim the internet for short articles on time management (since we long ago gave up on reading whole books). Sometimes we decide to get up earlier or stay up later, hoping to add another hour or two of productivity to our lives. Since we can't add more hours to the day, we try to change ourselves. We try to do more, to be more.

As part of that process, we often draw attention to how much TV Americans watch or how much time is spent surfing the internet or scrolling through social media. But what if our problem is not time management? *What if, rather than causing our problems, endless TV watching and internet surfing are signs of a deeper malady?* Maybe this escapism reveals a sickness in our souls that we have been neglecting.

I think we have a massive problem, but it is not a time-management issue. It is a *pastoral* and a *theological* problem: *we do not understand the blessings of our God-given limits.* As we will discover over the next forty days, better understanding God, ourselves, and what God expects of us can be truly liberating. This is an invitation to a more humane path: I invite you on this journey with me.

QUESTIONS FOR REFLECTION

- In what ways do you feel endlessly stretched and overwhelmed?
- Now that you have considered the problems you can't solve—which can be a pretty tense exercise—set those problems aside for a moment, take a deep breath, and meditate on the following: Jesus tells us, "Come to me, all who labor and are heavy laden,

and I will give you rest. Take my yoke upon you, and learn from me, for I am gentle and lowly in heart, and *you will find rest for your souls*. For my yoke is easy, and my burden is light" (Matt. 11:28–30). What does this passage tell us about Jesus? Who is the source of rest? Is Jesus someone you could relax with?

- What do you think God expects of you in a given day? A week? A year? A lifetime? Take time to candidly write down your thoughts as you consider these questions. Also, consider jotting down what unspoken "expectations" you think God has for you. What expectations of yourself might not be from God? The results might surprise you.

- If you could sit down with Jesus and have a relaxed conversation with him over coffee, what would he say about these expectations? How would he talk about your limited time and energy, your finite emotional resilience and resources? In what ways might it be hard to open your heart and receive these words of encouragement from your gentle Savior?

Finitude Is Not Sin

How I spend this ordinary day in Christ is how I will spend
my Christian life.

—Tish Harrison Warren, *Liturgy of the Ordinary*

"Finitude" is a fancy word we don't use a lot in our day, but it
simply means "limits." Put simply, *to be finite is to be limited
in space, time, knowledge, energy, and perspective.* In Christian terminology, this is just another way of saying "creature,"
since, by definition, we all are finite. Only God the Creator is
infinite. But appreciating our creaturely limits has always been
a challenge for our species.

Though humans were the pinnacle of God's creation, Adam
and Eve became dissatisfied, rejecting divine generosity and
warnings by grasping after power they could not control. God
had given Adam and Eve the fullness of the garden and many
other rich gifts; accordingly, the original sin has the shape of
taking the one thing that was not given to them. Rather than
perceiving their divinely given limitation as a *good gift,* they
viewed it naively and greedily, as if it were cruel or overly re-
strictive, like children doubting the wisdom of a parent who

tells them not to stick a finger into an electrical outlet. Parents do not set such limits because they disrespect or hate their children; rather, they do so because they love them and recognize the danger of ignoring their natural limits. The shock could kill them!

Thus, Genesis 3 onward tells of our discomfort with any divine restrictions and our rebellion against God's wisdom. As Old Testament scholar Gerhard von Rad observes concerning Genesis 3, "A movement began in which man pictures himself as growing more and more powerful, more and more titanic,"[1] producing a distorted and destructive view of personal power. In fact, the Genesis narrative presents a turning from the original, good ordering of creation to a disordering. We reject shalom, and that affects everything. Denying our limits disorders our relationships with God, our neighbors, and the rest of creation.

This challenge is not just about God putting external limits on us (e.g., "Do not murder"), but also about how he designed us. We simply can't help everyone, know all the answers, or do everything. We were never made to be able to "do it all."

No level of time management can put more hours into the day. Our bodies, our minds, and our relationships reflect our created limits. Keep in mind that "finite" here doesn't necessarily imply sin and death: even before sin or the fall, Adam and Eve were limited, since simply being *creatures* implies limitation. In fact, being finite is part of our good—*it is how God made us.*

Christian concern with original sin or the fall certainly orders [our] mortal existence in new ways, but it does not alter the fundamental character of creatureliness.

—Ephraim Radner, *A Time to Keep: Theology, Mortality, and the Shape of Human Life* (Waco: Baylor University Press, 2016), 40.

Surely only somebody who'd failed to notice how remarkable it is that anything is, in the first place, would take their own being as such a given—as if it were something they had every right to have conferred upon them, and never to have taken away.

—Oliver Burkeman, *Four Thousand Weeks: Time Management for Mortals* (New York: Farrar, Straus & Giroux, 2021), 66.

How often do you and I feel like we are letting God down because we don't get more done each day? But *finitude is not sin*! Adam and Eve were created finite, and they were called "good." Yes, if you play video games for ten hours a day, you have a problem. But for many of you reading this devotional, your problem is a different one: you've started to imagine that you are lazy or negligent if you can't get the endless to-do list completed, never actually wondering whether that's realistic and never even asking whether God expects us to work like machines and endlessly produce. Maybe these unhealthy expectations about efficiency and endless productivity don't come from God but rather from distorting voices in our heads and in our culture.

We sometimes wrongly attribute all our problems to sin when in fact they are often a matter of running up against the limits inherent in being creatures rather than God. This is how the serpent tempted Eve, by leading her to doubt the goodness of her finitude. With his indirect tactics, the serpent has encouraged his hearers, both ancient and modern, to imagine that they can and should *know more*. They should not only do more but *be more*. The serpent implies that divinely given limits are a fault to overcome rather than a beneficial gift to be honored and received.

Because of the fall, we all live with a disordered view of our healthy limits. Therefore, we need to appreciate anew the goodness of being creatures, which includes our physical, mental, and emotional limits. Instead of feeling like we need to ask God's forgiveness for not being able to do everything, we may need to ask his forgiveness for ever imagining we could!

QUESTIONS FOR REFLECTION

- Return to Matthew 11:28–30, where Jesus says, "Come to me, all who labor and are heavy laden, and I will give you rest. Take my yoke upon you, and learn from me, for I am gentle and lowly in heart, and *you will find rest for your souls*. For my yoke is easy, and my burden is light." Do you see that kind of rest as a possibility for yourself, or do you simply have too much to do? How might this kind of rest ground you in your daily life?
- Can you identify some limitations that you have assumed result from sin, when in truth they are just part of your creaturely finitude?
- How might you learn to value the good of productivity, while also keeping your God-given limits in view? How might having a healthier appreciation for your finitude equip you to navigate your life a bit differently? How would you talk to Jesus about your limits? Are you comparing yourself and your life to others in a way that's not helpful? What might be God's assignment for you in this season?

Finitude as a Gift

We have no other experience of God but human experience. When I experience God, what sustains me is, at least first of all, God made human.

—Emmanuel Falque, *The Metamorphosis of Finitude*

Creaturely finitude necessarily frames what it means to love God and neighbor with our whole heart, soul, mind, and strength. Consequently, any attempt to understand how to live and love faithfully must consider that framework. The statements below can help show us the nature of our finitude and how love works in and through that finitude. Since these are some of the pivotal assumptions underlying future reflections, I encourage you to read through them slowly, trying to consider the effects each one has on Christian expectations and experience:

- God is the good Creator, who has designed us as good creatures—in fact, as "very good!"
- Part of the good of being a creature is having limits.

- The incarnation (i.e., the Son becoming fully human) is God's great yes to his creation, including human limits.
- God has designed the person for the community and the community for the person.
- The creator God is also the Sustainer and Redeemer, so God's saving work doesn't undermine our creaturely value but reaffirms it.
- We are never asked to relate to God in any way other than as human creatures.
- God's goal for humanity is for us to become lovers of God, our neighbors, and the rest of creation.

Once we see ourselves within this framework—where our creaturely finitude plays a good and essential part of our being and experience—we begin to view pressures and endless expectations differently. We start to relate to God and others in a more fruitful way, not seeking an infinite capacity. After all, only God has infinite capacities! We worship him as he has made us—as dignified, purposeful, vulnerable, and finite creatures. We do not apologize for our creaturely needs and dependence on others; this is how God has made us, and it is good.

We've already asked, "Am I enough?" If we are ever to answer that question well, we must ask the central question, "What

> *Radical* is the sort of word many Christians like. Radical faith. Radical church. Radical discipleship. Radical mission. But I wonder if radical faith is the correct antidote to a boring, stale faith. . . . The call to be radical can—whether intentionally or unintentionally—denigrate the significance of the ordinary. . . . One of the most radical lifestyles is to stay rooted and attentive to beauty within the ordinary.
>
> —Wesley Vander Lugt, *Beauty Is Oxygen: Finding a Faith That Breathes* (Grand Rapids: Eerdmans, 2024), 108–9.

does God think of me—not of generic humanity but of *me*, in my singularity, my particularity, my smallness?" In other words, "How do I relate to Christ without ceasing to be me?" We will explore this question more fully in the next few days. But for now, consider meditating on a summation of what I am advocating here, which hopefully not only reinforces what we have already said but also points to where we are going: *God delights in our finitude. He is not embarrassed or shocked by our creatureliness. Since he is not apologetic about it, we should stop apologizing for it ourselves. As we will see, our sin is a problem, but being a creature and having limits is not.* We need to appreciate the reality of being human as *good*!

To start affirming our creaturely finitude as a good quality rather than an evil to be overcome, we must confess that God loves me and not just Christ instead of me. His love is not driven by ignorance, but by delight and purpose. God likes how he made you. It's *sin* that is the problem! It distorts who we were meant to be, and because we now sin we have a real problem. But we too often get confused here. God doesn't love us *because* of Christ's work or the Spirit's renewing presence; Calvary and Pentecost are evidence of the *overflow* of God's love for us, not the basis of it. The Son and Spirit do not convince the Father to love us, but they are the greatest possible manifestations of divine love and concern for us.

More on this in the coming days.

QUESTIONS FOR REFLECTION

- Do you consider your finitude a gift? Why or why not?
- If your finitude is a gift from God, what would it mean to give it back to him? In what ways might your actions or ways of navigating life demonstrate a denial of the goodness of your finitude? How might such a denial

relate to the way God has created you (e.g., with respect to your introversion or extroversion, physical limitations, and seasons of life)?

- How might the truth that we're made in God's image change our perception of ourselves?
- Have you ever thought that Jesus was trying to convince the Father to love people, rather than displaying the Father's already existent love? How might this misunderstanding challenge one's time with God?

Does God Love . . . Me?

The indwelling Christ enables each person to be more himself
than he was ever able to be before.

—Frederica Mathewes-Green, *Praying the Jesus Prayer*

A fair place to begin thinking about the goodness of human
finitude is by understanding the importance of our particularity. We are often far more uncomfortable with who we are than
we may at first realize.

If you ask most Christians whether God loves them, they
don't normally hesitate to answer yes, maybe even enthusiastically. But are we simply repeating an automatic "right answer"
that doesn't truly reflect our internal world? Often lurking
under such quick responses are deep and abiding insecurities
about God's attitude toward us. Consequently, asking a different question has often yielded a more revealing answer, which
can open up a compelling conversation. *Does God like you?*

"Love" is a beautiful word. Said in the right context and by the
right person, it can still bring goosebumps to the most hardened
person, enliven the saddest soul, and calm the angriest heart. Love
draws together, unites, and heals. God's love animates the entire
gospel story, making it good news for us sinners. Love—true and

real love—is cool water for a parched soul, food for the hungry, and welcome for the stranger. God's love makes the world go round and sustains it despite human sin and cosmic brokenness.

However, we have so often heard of God's love that the word bounces off us like a marshmallow. When it hits us, it feels so light we are not sure it has actually touched us. We know we are supposed to believe and affirm that God loves us, but most of us have serious doubts about it.

What about the word "like"? I like cheesecake. I like a cool spring morning. I like leaning back at the table after a meal with my wife and adult children, listening to their adventures and their painfully accurate teasing of me. I like sitting around a campfire with my friends Jay and Jeffrey, eating, drinking, and filling the evening with ridiculous laughter, philosophical reflections, and tear-inducing stories. "Like" often carries with it a sense of preference, inclination, and delight, as when a woodworker looks at the gorgeous table she built and says, "Oh, I like that. That is really good. I want that in my house."

Have you ever felt that your parents, your spouse, or your God loved you, while wondering whether they actually *liked* you? "Love" is so loaded with obligations and duty that it often loses much of its emotive force, its pleasure and satisfaction. "Like," though, can remind us of an aspect of God's love that we far too easily forget.

Forgetting that God likes us stunts our ability to enjoy his love. But remembering that God likes us allows us to receive his joy and delight. Forgiveness—as beautiful and crucial as it is—is not enough. Unless forgiveness is understood to come

> The gospel is this: We are more sinful and flawed in ourselves than we ever dared believe, yet at the very same time we are more loved and accepted in Jesus Christ than we ever dared hope.
>
> —Timothy Keller, *The Meaning of Marriage: Facing the Complexities of Commitment with the Wisdom of God* (New York: Penguin, 2013), 44.

from love and lead back to love, unless we understand the gospel in terms of God's fierce delight in us and not merely a wiping away of offenses, unless we understand God's battle for us as a dramatic personal rescue and not merely a cold forensic process, we have ignored most of Scripture as well as the needs of the human condition. We are forgetting how good and loving our Creator is. In order to return to a proper perspective, we need to look intently at Jesus, who perfectly expresses the will and delights of our heavenly Father.

QUESTIONS FOR REFLECTION

- What do you imagine God sees in you? While he can't delight in your sin, can you imagine he still delights in you, his beautiful creation? Can you imagine him not just loving you, but even *liking* you? What aspects of you do you think God doesn't like?

- What pieces of your particularity have you sought to get rid of but, you now understand, simply reflect how God has made you? Can you embrace both your strengths and weaknesses as gifts of love?

- It might be easy for you to list your sins and shortcomings. But can you name some things about yourself that you think reveal God's love and delight in you? If you only imagine negative or bad things about yourself, could it be that you are struggling to see some of the good in God's creation, his specific creation of you?

- Mark 10:13–16 describes Jesus interacting with children. Do you suppose these children were standing still, in awe of him and afraid to move or laugh? What does "like a child" in verse 15 mean if not "uninhibited," "exuberant," or "without pretense"? Jesus seems to have liked them very much. What could you say to Jesus that would be true to the core of your being and not hidden by politeness?

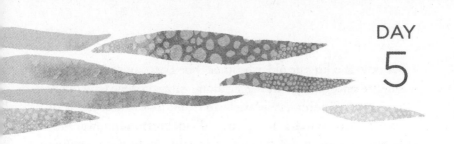

Does God See . . . Me?

The unholy is the absurd affair in which the creature seeks to be a creature in a way other than that which is purposed by God.
—John Webster, *Holiness*

Some traditions place so much emphasis on our identity as "sinners" that they reserve no room for our deeper identity as the creatures whom God designed in his own image to experience life in warmth and fellowship. We were meant to experience his original delight in us, with our particular spunk, our personality, and our differences. Instead, we've learned that God, like our parents, *has* to love us (or so we've been told). That's just part of the arrangement. This reality too often works solely in terms of obligations and our failure to meet them; we absorb the idea that God thinks and acts only in terms of obligation too. Thus, we can misperceive God's love (and law) as we misperceive our parents' love, believing it consists largely of self-imposed (even arbitrary) obligations and tit-for-tat responses.

Maybe the best we can hope for is that God will put up with us if we keep our heads down and hang around Jesus. We imagine that God's acceptance of us is like that of a host of a party we attend with our older brother. The host can only tolerate our presence because we tagged along with someone he actually delights in (in this case, Jesus). In truth, that is how many of us experience God's "love": mere divine toleration toward us. Some versions of this type of spirituality attempt to comfort believers by telling them that since they are covered in Christ's blood, God doesn't really see them (since they are sinners) but only sees Christ (since he alone is free from sin). In this version, God really doesn't want to look at you. Or maybe he just can't.

It's entirely understandable (and a symptom of growth) if the person who has heard versions of this message for years—maybe even decades—works up enough courage to ask, "If God only sees me in Christ, does he even see *me*? Does he know *me*? How can I say God loves me? Maybe he just loves his Son?"

Sometimes it is the non-Christian who is first to raise these awkward questions. Looking at the Christian faith, they ask, "Do I have to stop being *me* in order to become a Christian?" Answering this question may be trickier than most people realize. Dismissing such questions as self-absorbed or individualistic is often just a way of avoiding them.

Too often, in some portrayals of the gospel, we are presented with a wrathful Father and a loving Christ. In this way, the

---

Jesus looks at us and he knows we cannot help ourselves. He looks at us this very day [Good Friday] in the same way he looked at every human being that he encountered during his earthly life: with infinite sadness for our predicament, yet with unquenchable love and with unflinching resolve to rescue us from certain condemnation and death, whatever it took, wherever it led, whatever the price. "Self-help" is crucified with Christ—for as St. Paul writes, "While we were still helpless, Christ died for the ungodly" (Rom. 5:6).

—Fleming Rutledge, *The Undoing of Death: Sermons for Holy Week and Easter* (Grand Rapids: Eerdmans, 2002), 220–21.

Father appears as an easily offended, furious perfectionist who is only persuaded to forgive by means of his more compassionate Son. The Father is now willing to put up with us—but only because Jesus loves us. The obvious tension between the Father and the Son in such a story clearly violates the oneness of God and the many passages in the Bible that highlight the Father's own love (e.g., John 3:16; Neh. 9:17; Isa. 43:1–3; 54:10; Rom. 5:8; 2 Cor. 13:14; Eph. 2:4; 1 John 4:8).

Claims that God can't stand to be in the presence of sin are fundamentally opposed to the gospel and the nature of God. This claim and its many variants are backward: it's sin that can't stand the presence of God. Sin cannot claim leverage over God. This view of God as irritable makes him out to be the kind of being who doesn't have a beloved at all, except perhaps himself. It undercuts and denies the divinity of Christ, who as God incarnate was present with and attentive to sinners his whole life. It misunderstands the Holy Spirit, who comes to dwell *in* sinners in order to make them saints. This misunderstanding can develop from the sort of theology that views justice only in terms of retribution, with little concern for restoration.

The truth is, redemption is not just for some generic humanity but for particular persons: the Shepherd knows his sheep, he lays down his life for them, and he calls them by name (John 10:3, 11, 14).

QUESTIONS FOR REFLECTION

- Have you understood Christ dying on your behalf differently from the way discussed here? How might the belief that our heavenly Father delights in you (which is why he deals with your sin on your behalf!) change your view of yourself?

- Take a moment to think about God seeing you as you fully are (with your quirks, personality, preferences, etc.). How does this change how you think he views you? How does it change how you view yourself? Maybe being a faithful Christian doesn't mean you have to change your personality.
- How does God's true sight change your perception of others?
- Jesus once said, "Whoever has seen me has seen the Father" (John 14:9). What was Jesus's attitude toward the sinners around him (i.e., everybody else)? What does this say about the Father's attitude toward you?

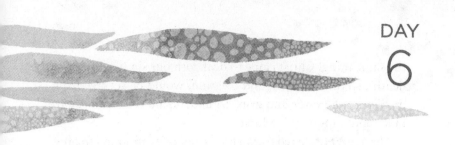

New Creatures

Unified, Living, and Believing

I have been crucified with Christ. It is no longer I who live, but Christ who lives in me. And the life I now live in the flesh I live by faith in the Son of God, who loved me and gave himself for me.

—Galatians 2:20

Galatians 2:20 is one of the most memorized New Testament texts, but that doesn't prevent it from being misunderstood and misapplied. What is Paul arguing here, and what is he not advocating? Given the language about death in this verse, some people interpret it as meaning that I need to stop being me and you need to stop being you, as if we must all conform to some generic Christian personality or ideal. Maybe everyone needs to wear khakis or dresses, listen to the same music, and have the same sense of humor. But is that what "It is no longer I who live" implies? Such applications misunderstand both the singularity of Christ and the value of our created differences, which are good and not bad. We must learn to avoid confusing our creaturely particularity with sinfulness. They are not the same thing! Christ came to deal with our sin (i.e., put it to death), so that we, his good creation, would be set free from its distorting power and grip. To understand this, we need to talk about union with Christ.

Has it ever occurred to you how strange it can sound to non-Christians when Christians talk about Jesus? We don't merely talk about him as a great teacher of wisdom or an edgy sage or prophet; rather, we also talk about him as the very Son of God, who took on human nature, becoming like us in all ways except that he never sinned (1 John 1:1; Heb. 4:15). Christian worship around the globe centers on understanding him as the Messiah, and we make claims far more world-shaking than calling him a teacher of wisdom or powerful prophet. Believers claim that we somehow continue, personally and corporately, to have fellowship with this man and benefit from his life, death, resurrection, ascension, and ongoing intercession in heaven. We belong to him, and he belongs to us. This belonging is possible because of what we call our "union with Christ."

New Testament scholar Constantine R. Campbell nicely surveys the variety of imagery and language that the apostle Paul uses to frame a Christian vision of union with Christ, offering this conclusion: "A believer is united to Christ at the moment of coming to faith; their union is established by the indwelling of the Spirit. The person united to Christ therefore entered into participation with Christ in his death, resurrection, ascension, and glorification. As a participant in Christ's death and resurrection, the believer dies to the world and is identified with the realm

When the New Testament describes the Christian, it emphasizes, not the continued sinfulness of the believer, but his newness in Christ. Our self-image ought to reflect that emphasis.

—Anthony A. Hoekema, *The Christian Looks at Himself*
(Grand Rapids: Eerdmans, 1975), 73.

of Christ. As a member of the realm of Christ, the believer is incorporated into his body, since union with Christ entails union with his members."[1] Because of this union, we are genuinely made "new" in Christ. But we are made new not in the sense that I must stop liking coffee or change the color of my skin. No, this newness is really about God redeeming his good creatures who had fallen into the distorting grip of sin, death, and the devil.

John Calvin (1509–64) describes this unity by writing, "As long as Christ remains outside of us, and we are separated from him, all that he has suffered and done for the salvation of the human race remains useless and of no value for us."[2] But when the Spirit makes us new creatures in Christ, we are freed from sin's dominion and liberated to worship and enjoy our Lord as humanity was originally created to do. We do not perfectly experience the depth of this freedom and joy until glory, but even now, amid our different personalities and distinctives, we are "hidden with Christ in God" (Col. 3:3), secure in our relationship with the Creator and set free to truly love others as he has loved us.

As a believer, you are in Christ and Christ is in you. You are secure by the power of the Spirit, who applies the finished work of Christ to your life. The same Spirit who hovered over the waters to bring about order (Gen. 1:2) now empowers you to grow and blossom as the "real you." And being the real you ultimately means growing in communion with God and neighbor, just as God originally intended. But this isn't generic love or communion. It's particular. It's about you, me, and each of our neighbors. If we were no more than copies of a single pattern—just like everyone else—we would not have communion but an echo chamber. Believers united to Christ are connected yet distinct, each adding their unique voice and actions to the universe. God delights in you as you use the particular gifts he has given. You are a child of the King, so don't imagine you need to be someone else. Resist your sin, indeed. But don't confuse your particularity with sin. You don't have to cease being you, since your Creator likes what he has made. He just wants to free you from the sin that is distorting the goodness he intended when he made you.

QUESTIONS FOR REFLECTION

- How have you experienced the transforming work of God throughout your life, even if it seems small? What do you think about God "changing" you? Do you find yourself mostly resisting or actively engaging God's transforming work in your life? How might Galatians 2:20 influence your thinking?

- How might we think about Christ making us new, while still valuing our particularity or distinctiveness? What difference would it make to believe that sanctification is about God restoring our truest selves, not about him creating a different version that is not authentic? As we'll see later in this devotional, you are never more yourself than when you are experiencing love for God and neighbor and even rightly relating to the rest of creation.

- If we are to think of ourselves as children of the King, how should we imagine those in the church around us?

- We are not made to all look and act the same. Given that we are designed with our uniqueness and distinctive personalities for a reason, how might this reality change your view of yourself and others, including how you interact with your sisters and brothers in Christ? What are some unique things about yourself that you can rejoice in and embrace (but are not sinful), knowing that God created you like this?

- John 15:1–11 describes an organic, active, continuing relationship between Jesus and his followers. How does this passage represent unity with Christ while preserving the distinct identity of each of his followers?

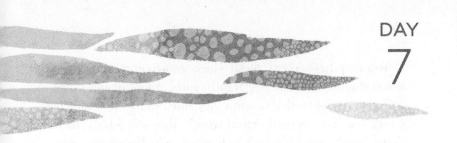

The Importance
of Our Physicality

> Though touch should be important for everyone, its importance
> should be especially clear for believers because our God made
> a touchable, material world. And he made humans within that
> world with five senses to purposefully engage it.
>
> —Lore Ferguson Wilbert, *Handle with Care*

How we view ourselves and others is inseparable from how we
perceive our bodies. Our flesh is not an insignificant, disposable
container carrying an internal spirit, although we are sometimes tempted to see the body as unimportant and only the
soul as valuable. All of us—young or old, quick or slow—are
embodied creatures located in real time and space: we are here
and not there, this body and not that one. Computer technology, because it tends to engage the mind rather than the whole
body, may allow us to hide behind avatars, but in real life, we
cannot escape our actual sweat glands, digestive tracts, or ner-
vous systems.

You may have heard about video game centers in South Korea that never close. Apparently, some young people come and stay for days—that is, until they smell so bad that they're kicked out. Lost in their digital worlds, they still inhabit their chairs, producing odors and body waste, whether they want to acknowledge it or not. Ignoring your body and pretending it is not you has detrimental effects on both you and others.

We all want to be loved. We—not just the idea of us, nor simply words about or by us, but we *in our totality*—need to be welcomed, known, and treasured. Under normal conditions, we experience this love of our whole selves through touch and communication, both of which are vital to our humanity.

The countless needs that human bodies have are intentional design elements put in place by our Creator. Furthermore, we were not made to be independent, lone wolves. Instead, God created us to be connected to each other and the rest of creation in a web of relationships and interdependence—not ghostly,

> Up from the bed of river
> God scooped the clay;
> And by the bank of the river
> He kneeled him down;
> And there the great God Almighty
> Who lit the sun and fixed it in the sky,
> Who flung the stars to the most far corner of the night,
> Who rounded the earth in the middle of his hand;
> This Great God,
> Like a mammy bending over her baby,
> Kneeled down in the dust
> Toiling over a lump of clay
> Till he shaped it in his own image
>
> —James Weldon Johnson, "The Creation," in *God's Trombones: Seven Negro Sermons in Verse* (New York: Penguin, 1927), 17.

> All creatures reflect the goodness of God simply in being what God gives them to be; humans, at their best, reflect the goodness of God by a self-conscious and freely chosen active alignment of what they are with God's gift-giving to them.
>
> —Kathryn Tanner, *Jesus, Humanity and the Trinity: A Brief Systematic Theology* (Minneapolis: Fortress, 2001), 70.

disembodied souls but dust-derived, Spirit-breathed creatures. *And this is good!* Our physicality opens us up to interactions with one another and with the world around us. Being human has always involved an embodied state, and that has always been a good, not a bad, thing.

Even dependence, contrary to the individualist philosophy of our culture, is part of the blessing of human existence. The first creation account in the Bible (Gen. 1) describes the entire material world as "good," but the second account (in Gen. 2) examines the creation of humanity in two parts. When it considers Adam as a creature to himself, "alone," the text declares this "not good" (2:18). Adam's body is not bad; his *aloneness* is the problem. So God responds by bringing Adam another like him, another who bears a body like his and yet is different. He doesn't bring the idea of another but rather the bodily presence of Eve. Adam experiences the goodness of creation when he depends on her.

We are designed for communion with one another, and our physicality supplies a medium for that communion. This communion itself exemplifies a need for God, our neighbors, and the earth. Genesis shows that physicality and its corresponding needs are not a flaw but a good element of God's original design. Sin and brokenness in the world, however, have twisted and undermined that goodness and have made us vulnerable to the manipulation of others. Consequently, we live in insecurity, simultaneously needing others and fearing that they won't accept us or may even abuse us. This precariousness drives us to pretend that we don't need others, but our attempts at self-sufficiency deny the relational nature of our being.

In order to understand our fundamental need for one another, we must keep returning to the question "Who am I?" Any answers to this question that ignore our bodies are neither realistic nor Christian.

Lilian Calles Barger reflects on our quickness to believe that we are not our bodies. We look into the mirror and think to ourselves, "This isn't who I am." A truly Christian spirituality, however, must always be a body-affirming spirituality. Barger comments, Christian spirituality "must provide freedom—not from the body, but to imagine what is possible even within the body's limitations." Whether one believes or rejects the Christian faith, spiritual practices always involve bodily practices. "My actions and work in the world are done through and in my body; the truest test of what I profess to be. What we need is a spirituality that honors the body we have and comprehends its social meaning but does not reduce us to it."[1]

Gaining a healthy appreciation for the ways our embodiment limits us will prove vital in developing a truly Christian vision of faithfulness that, in its realism, affirms the goodness of our physical bodies and how God has created us.

QUESTIONS FOR REFLECTION

- In what ways might we in the church misrepresent the Christian life by downplaying our embodiment? Why would God make us material beings? What about our physicality reflects the Creator?
- Read Matthew 6:25–33. According to this passage, how much and in what ways does God care for you physically?

- Although God doesn't need us to be professional athletes or supermodels, our physicality matters. Are you neglecting your body's needs for rest, good nutrition, and movement in this season of life? If so, what do you think is the underlying reason? What might be a realistic and healthy way to stop ignoring your embodiment?

- If holistic love involves physicality, how do we care for those who have experienced trauma or physical assault? How do we care for them if they are not ready to be touched but still require love?

- After losing a loved one, it's hard to accept that they are no longer around to hug, to see sitting at the dinner table, or to laugh with about an awkward moment. How well do we allow people to grieve the absence of dearly loved ones' bodies?

Today's Oversexualized Body

> For though we aren't our bodies, yet of nothing on earth do we
> have more intimate possession than these. Only through these
> do we dwell here.
>
> —Nicholas Wolterstorff, *Lament for a Son*

We live within a strange incongruity: On the one hand, we hear strident voices claiming that human bodies matter—in fact, maybe they are all that matter. Yet the bodies on our screens and billboards are usually well under thirty, tight-skinned, and with a perfect complexion, even when they are presented as grungy. They rarely look like most of us—the viewers who are absorbing the images. Add to that the fact that the image (whether of a man or a woman) is almost always sexualized, whether the model has juice from a burger running down her lips or he is in the middle of a tire commercial flirting with the viewer. In our cultural moment in the West, bodies are almost always reduced to sexuality. Is this how I am supposed to see myself and relate to others—always in a strongly sexualized manner?

Given our shared obsession with beautiful, culturally defined bodies in advertisements and entertainment, no critic can

The question of human limits, of the proper definition and place of human beings within the order of Creation, finally rests upon our attitude toward our biological existence, the life of the body in this world. What value and respect do we give to our bodies?

—Wendell Berry, "The Body and the Earth," in *The Art of the Commonplace: The Agrarian Essays of Wendell Berry,* ed. Norman Wirzba (Washington, DC: Shoemaker & Hoard, 2002), 93.

accuse American culture of being squeamish about the human body, right? Aren't the people who raise such questions simply to be dismissed as "puritanical"? And yet, even among the irreligious and those who have never heard of the Puritans, plenty of evidence exists of widespread embarrassment and unease with our own bodies. I'm too tall or short, too round or skinny, too dark or pale, too _____. You fill in the blank.

Bodies, we are tempted to believe, must always be ready for the judgment of public viewing. Bodily change in the process of aging is something we are constantly told to fight and overcome. One article confidently proclaims, "Fifty is the new thirty."[1] Postpartum women face endless ads to get their prepregnancy bodies back, often through surgery, so they will show little to no signs of change. Might this expectation and pressure not underestimate the power and significance of giving birth and creating new flesh out of your very own body? We want to erase the marks of real humanity and change from our bodies to fit a societal image of perfection and flawlessness—again, almost always idealizing youth. Ongoing unrealistic expectations often breed a toxic impulse to compare ourselves to others. As a result, our self-image and our relationships suffer.

Most people know that women are often viewed as sexualized objects and that such a reality imposes significant personal and social pressures on them, depersonalizing them and overwhelming them with unrealistic expectations. But recent research shows that men are increasingly presented as sexualized objects and are beginning to feel these pressures as well.

Growing evidence suggests that negative body-image issues affect women and men alike. Ironically, some have apparently started to believe that public objectification of the male figure is a sign of progress. Instead of liberation, however, we find that male body dissatisfaction is spiking among those who internalize sociocultural ideals, producing a rough equivalent to female body dissatisfaction. Rather than correcting the degrading objectification of women—which seems to be a never-ending battle—we have apparently decided we should just give men the same treatment. This way we can all grow in our insecurity together!

As a result, we now reduce both men and women to objects of desire or repulsion, rather than treating them as whole human beings who have dignity and worth. At the risk of sounding like a grumpy old man, I find it strange—but no longer surprising—that, while prominent voices in the entertainment industry bemoan rampant sexism (a *very* legitimate concern!), that same industry as a whole continues to promote unrealistic physical stereotypes and an objectification that feeds rather than fights the problem. Instead of honoring the whole human person, it exalts artificial and digitally manufactured images. It promotes a simulated, distorted cultural ideal rather than a realistic, healthy view of actual earthly flesh and blood.

Although we are sexual creatures, our sexual desires and urges don't tell the full story of our body's importance. Objecting to current cultural trends doesn't mean that we hate our bodies; rather, it means that we have a more profound respect for them. God likes us, and that includes our bodies—we are embodied creatures by his own good design. While it may sound strange to some, one of the most spiritual things you can do as a Christian is to grow more comfortable with your embodiment rather than to feel shame about it. If this sounds outrageous or strange, it's worth taking some time to consider why that is the case.

QUESTIONS FOR REFLECTION

- In an age when bodies are so often sexualized, can you recall a moment you felt known and loved, body and soul, in a nonsexual context? Recall a memory of positive physical touch. How did that touch affirm you as an embodied child or adult?

- Why do you think we find it so difficult to feel comfortable in our own skin? When we don't feel that way, how might that affect our relationship with God and others?

- Luke 23:50–56 describes the disciples' burial arrangements for Jesus's body. What details are given about those arrangements in this passage? What does this tell us about their respect for the human body in general?

- God is good, and he gives us good gifts, including sex. What might it look like to have a healthy view of human bodies, a view that recognizes our sexuality without the oversexualization we so often find in our day?

Who Am I?
Why Does My Body Matter?

The physical presence of other Christians is a source of incomparable joy and strength to the believer.

—Dietrich Bonhoeffer, *Life Together*

So who am I? How should I relate to you? We must resist the temptation either to disparage people's bodies or to idealize them. The former action undermines the goodness of our creatureliness, whereas the latter increases our distance from the real people in front of us. Similarly, we must reject the trendy narrative that tells us that our sexual desires are the most important thing about us, just as we should reject the claim that our sexuality is inherently evil. Obviously, land mines are everywhere in this discussion, but my main goal here is to help us recognize our discomfort with our physicality; we need to affirm what God has called good. Our bodies and their inherent limits are a good gift from our good Creator.

We can always improve ourselves and always look better, can't we? And that reality's not all bad. Faithfully caring for our bodies is good. In this way, we properly care for ourselves. But we need to

If God became man in Christ, then Christ participates, as does each of us, in the dust, in the galaxies, in the atom, in the animal world, in everything which belongs to the created world. He has taken upon himself the experience of all createdness. He is one of us, but in him everything created can see itself, having reached the final term of its vocation and growth.

—Metropolitan Anthony of Sourozh, *The Living Body of Christ*
(London: Darton, Longman & Todd, 2008), 129.

ask what underlies many of our desires to improve. Except when speaking to tweens and teenagers, we tend not to use the language of "acceptance," but all of us, regardless of age, struggle at times to feel comfortable in our literal skin. We want to belong, to be welcomed, to be accepted, to be smiled at. Does our instinct to suck in our gut and avoid shirts with horizontal stripes point to insecurities about our bodies? *Our problem is not just what others think of us but what we think of ourselves.* We must come to terms with our physicality and our respective versions of it. Maybe this will provoke some of us to eat less, some of us to eat more. But all bodies need food and friends, for without sustenance and the acceptance of others, both body and soul begin to wither.

A healthy view of our bodies appreciates the real, the particular, and the commonplace. We are called to affirm our creaturely existence in its distinctiveness, seeing it as a blessing rather than a curse. As we will explore more in later devotions, our bodies both unite us to the whole of humanity and are crucial to our particularity. They are not meant for shame but for relationship, health, and faithfulness.

Again, who am I? Who are you? To fully know me is to know the physical person sitting or standing in your presence; it is to listen to the sound of my voice as it moves the tiny bones in your ear canal. Our bodies both distinguish us and allow us to come together.

At the core of this Christian vision is a particular human being, a first-century Jewish man, the son of Mary, the final Adam. Here was a man who knew the realities of time and space pushing against his body. Here was a vulnerable baby, a prepubescent boy, a developing teenager, a hammer-holding young adult, and eventually an animated teacher. Here was a sinless one, Jesus of Nazareth, born and dwelling in real time and space, with fingers, knees, and taste buds. Here was a man with a real body, real restrictions, real curves, and real birthmarks. Before his ascension, he knew and related to other humans through the physical space-time medium of their bodily presence. In this way, he didn't negate their humanity but instead affirmed their physicality, healed them, and restored relationships in the process.

QUESTIONS FOR REFLECTION

- John 5:1–9 records the healing of the lame man at the pool of Bethesda. The passage turns on the change of the man's physical condition. How does the man's lameness affect his relations with others? How does his physical healing affect those relationships?
- Has someone made you feel known and loved through the way they recognized you, in both soul and body? Why is this type of knowing deeper than purely non-physical knowing?
- Bodies are unique and particular. Why do we imagine that an "ideal" body exists? Are you satisfied with your own body? Notice your reaction when you encounter another's physicality. Do you tend to idealize or judge others? Be aware of your internal attitudes toward others and, therefore, yourself.
- How might internalizing the reality of Jesus's body change how you view your own body?

Embodied Worship

For it is in and through our God-given bodies that worship
and mission, work and play, relationship and service are fully
realized.

—W. David O. Taylor, *A Body of Praise*

Standing next to the soccer field with little kids jumping
around—the motion was too random to be called "running"—
I had a great conversation with a friend who is an accomplished
physician. She had grown up in the church and continued there
as an adult believer, so she is deeply aware of both the strengths
of church culture and its weaknesses. This awareness has given
her insightful questions and a sense of uneasiness. In our conversation, she decided to be candid with me about her experience:
"To be honest, in recent years, I've often felt like my time in yoga
class has been more meaningful to me than going to church.
I don't know, the bodily experiences there often just resonate
with me in a way I rarely experience at church." As the sun was
shining on this cool, crisp morning, her comments prompted
my curiosity. I kept asking questions and listening. Her story,
like the stories of many others, pointed to a fairly common challenge that many people face, including myself. Put succinctly, at

church she felt as if she was reduced to a brain on a stick, simply there to receive information. Sit, listen, take notes, and then go home ready to try harder for another week. She felt that her yoga class treated her as a whole person, engaging her body, mind, and will. Often, she found quiet and reflection more valued in her stretching sessions than they were in the sacred space of the church. Conversations like this make me wonder how we have lost sight of the importance of our physical presence in worship.

When a church service feels more like attending a lecture than being physically engaged in worship before the triune God, should we really be surprised that we feel disconnected? I'm a Presbyterian, and we love lectures. We tend to attract ministers and members who place great emphasis on the intellect—it is one of the great gifts of the tradition. We are (or so we suppose) a reasonable people. Yet this inclination has also been one of the great dangers throughout our history. In our appreciation of the mind, we often can end up (unintentionally?) acting as if our minds are all that matter—as if even our thoughts can be disconnected from our experiences as physical creatures in a material world. This partiality to devaluing our bodies distorts our view of God, ourselves, and life in this world.

Take corporate worship, for example. Have you ever noticed how much of the biblical material associated with worship emphasizes our physicality—eat the bread (1 Cor. 11:23–24), drink the wine (11:25–26), clap your hands (Ps. 47:1), lift them in prayer (1 Tim. 2:8), fill your lungs and cry out to God (Ps. 95:1–2), bow down and kneel (95:6), anoint with oil (James 5:14), and baptize

> Worship is the heart of discipleship if and only if worship is a repertoire of Spirit-endued practices that grab hold of your gut, recalibrate your *kardia*, and capture your imagination.
>
> —James K. A. Smith, *You Are What You Love: The Spiritual Power of Habit* (Grand Rapids: Brazos, 2016), 83.

with water (Matt. 3:11)? Worship in the Bible engages all five senses: sight, touch, smell, taste, and hearing. Such worship cannot be fully experienced by sitting on the couch in front of a TV or listening to a podcast. Sure, in some cases, especially for the sick and homebound, television and podcasts are a genuine gift. But whether we think of the midcentury trend of drive-in church services, or the many believers who continue to watch online "church" but are in no way immunocompromised, or claims that one can worship God just as well alone on a ski slope, each of these can play into the individualistic errors of our culture and deny the vision of worship presented in the Old and New Testaments. Corporate worship is meant to foster communion with God and neighbor, and when we are not physically together, we are increasingly tempted to reduce Christianity to mental assent rather than viewing it as a way of life together.

In Saudi Arabia, for example, believers have long praised God for broadcast services on the radio and the internet, making more connections possible. But their deeper hope and yearning has always been for an opportunity to, without fear or hesitation, warmly embrace other believers in the flesh. Those of us who live in lands that honor religious liberty too easily forget the value of connecting our bodies and worship.

When we gather for worship, we—our physical selves—engage one another to receive strength, to meet one another, to meet Jesus, and to be sent out into the world renewed in God's presence, love, and healing grace. God's love gathers many people into a unified body of diverse members, not to be disconnected individuals. Paul declares, "So in Christ we, though many, form one body, and each member belongs to all the others" (Rom. 12:5 NIV). Our bodies come together to make one body, and here, in response to the forgiveness and enlivening grace of God, we are given acceptance, courage, and hope. We feast on the bread and the wine, the body and the blood of Christ; these embodied realities affect us to our gut. Jesus as the bread of life and the living water reminds us of our absolute dependence on him and our continued reliance on his corporate body. We were created for healthy interdependence, but strands of our culture tempt us to imagine that maturity looks like total independence. Dependent on his body and blood, all believers are united in Christ—not just spiritually, but physically. Our corporate worship time together changes us, and part of the way we are changed is through the way the church treats our physicality.

QUESTIONS FOR REFLECTION

- Have you ever considered corporate worship as an embodied experience? In what ways do you use your body during worship? How might you become more aware of your physical experience during corporate worship?
- Read Psalm 95. Notice the physical actions involved in worship there. What would worship be like without those actions? List the actions, imagine yourself carrying them out in worship, and ask yourself what difference they would make.
- Think about Jesus entering a synagogue or engaging in prayer. How might imagining Jesus's physicality in worship ground our own practices and imagination when it comes to worship? Think of the ways he engaged with others physically during his earthly ministry (e.g., touching the sick or dead bodies and engaging with women or foreigners). In what ways was this engagement radical in first-century Jewish culture? In what ways might Jesus be a model for how we interact with others today?
- Take a moment and pray for those in the persecuted church who have no opportunity to gather physically for worship.

The Holy Kiss

But to love oneself in the divine sense is to love God, and truly
to love another person is to help that person to love God or in
loving God.

—Søren Kierkegaard, *Works of Love*

Greeting one another with a "holy kiss" or a "kiss of love" appears as a command surprisingly often in the New Testament (Rom. 16:16; 1 Cor. 16:20; 2 Cor. 13:12; 1 Thess. 5:26; 1 Pet. 5:14). Uninformed outsiders who heard this kind of language from the ancient church sometimes accused believers of orgies and sexual misconduct. However, rather than yield to this kind of misrepresentation, believers kept this affectionate gesture—beyond the immediate family—as a strong (physical) mark of Christian unity and love. Former strangers and even enemies, upon conversion, treated each other as brothers and sisters. No sociocultural pressures were to divide what God had joined together: rich and poor, Greek and non-Greek, male and female, young and old, slave and free, all assembled together as the new family of God (Rom. 3:29; Gal. 3:28; Col. 3:11).

Just as family members embrace one another before departing after a holiday feast, so the ancient church believed that corporate prayers should sometimes end with a kiss that "sealed the prayer" in Christian unity. Tertullian (160–240), for example, warns of those who have started to "withhold the kiss of peace (which is the seal of [corporate] prayer)." And then he adds, "What prayer is complete if separated from the holy kiss?"[1] Prayers were not simply the exercises of isolated individuals but the acts of physical human creatures who came together to worship.

Similarly, by the eighth century, when the divine liturgy was celebrated in Constantinople, in the great church of Hagia Sophia, "the holy kiss was initiated immediately before reciting the creed," when congregants were called to a shared belief and a mutual love, sealed by this kiss of peace.[2]

Given the possibility of abuse, however, the church also issued warnings about not exploiting or misapplying this intimate gesture. So, for example, even when it was still largely considered important, the Apostolic Constitutions (ca. 390) called for the division of "the Lord's kiss" among the sexes (women to women, men to men), as a way of protecting against any misuse. Although aware of the dangers and seeking to address them, the ancient church still sought to affirm physical embrace and warm hospitality, all with integrity and dignity.

> Until this point in my adult life, I had never actually been aware of my body from the inside. I was a floating head. Most of the time, it seemed like nothing existed from my jawline down. If something bodily did exist, I only knew how to scrutinize it as if detached, and from the outside.
>
> —Hillary McBride, *The Wisdom of Your Body: Finding Healing, Wholeness, and Connection through Embodied Living* (Grand Rapids: Brazos, 2021), 9–10.

Reacting against the widespread physical exploitation of the underclasses by the powerful, the early church stood out as a refuge for women and the poor. These people knew the church as a place where they were welcomed and treated on an equal level with all other believers, instead of being exploited (cf. James 2:1–9). It was a space where they could experience healthy, mutual dependence and love in moments of shalom that were characteristic of the original Eden. Historians have observed how the unifying expression of embrace and shared dignity was a crucial part of the church's explosive growth in its early centuries.[3]

Such gestures may seem silly or unnecessary at first, but I can assure you, they are most definitely not. Our historical moments and cultures may differ, but the underlying significance of such gestures has not dissipated. Whether we realize it or not, appropriate physical greetings connect our embodiment and therefore our full selves to this context of worship. They help integrate our lives and protect us from unhealthy divisions between body and soul, the physical and the spiritual, and creation and redemption. Short and tall, slender and robust, old and young, clever and simple, all are brought together and treated as one body in Christ through embrace, acceptance, and dignified love. Such action tells us, at a visceral level, that our bodies are important and loved, that we are important and loved, and that neither our bodies nor our whole selves can be reduced to sexuality or any other single appetite. Rather, our whole selves are welcomed, loved, and then sent out renewed in the peace of the Lord.

QUESTIONS FOR REFLECTION

- Consider the way you have experienced greeting times at church. What do you feel about the physicality of these interactions (or the lack thereof)? Do you feel comfortable embracing your neighbor, or would you rather stay on your side of the pew?

- How might greetings be done in a culturally sensitive way that still encourages healthy appreciation for our physicality and fellowship in corporate worship?

- John 13:5–17 describes the time when Jesus washed his disciples' feet. The social awkwardness of his action emphasizes the lessons he was teaching. How would you have felt if you had been sitting there and he began to wash your feet? How would you feel about washing someone else's feet? What kinds of spiritual and social meanings underlie this action, especially in light of this passage?

- As we saw on day 8, much of contemporary culture pushes us to oversexualize the body. How has your experience in the church countered or reaffirmed such oversexualization? The church is supposed to feel safe, like a family made up of mothers and fathers, sisters and brothers. How have you seen the church treat our bodies well? When or how has the church fallen short?

Jesus and Healthy Physical Touch

God made us with bodies and came in a body and died in a body and rose again in a body, and one day all His people will dwell with Him forever—every one of us in our own glorified body.
—Lore Ferguson Wilbert, *Handle with Care*

Do you know one of the main things my students will miss most when they graduate from college? It's not the cafeteria food or endless homework. It's something they probably don't even know they currently enjoy every day—physical touch! It's fairly common to see college students happily squish tightly next to a friend on a sofa, lay their heads on one another, fall laughingly into each other's arms, or playfully wrestle on the grass. But far too often, when students leave college, the daily physical contact dries up. They didn't even realize how much they enjoyed an embrace, a subtle affirming touch, the physical presence of another.

Appropriate(!) physical touch is crucial to human wholeness. Our bodies are meant to establish, sustain, and encourage

49

mutual relationships. Each of us was made for communion with others like us, and without such communion, we experience the isolation and solitude that easily breed loneliness and despair. Human communion often calls for healthy touch.

Renowned psychologist Bessel van der Kolk explains, "The most natural way that we humans calm down our distress is by being touched, hugged, and rocked."[1] This points to something primal in us—not to a flaw, but to the good work of our Creator. We were made for mutual embrace. Sadly, in our fallen world, which suffers the twisting effects of sin, these needs can be co-opted and betrayed.

When those in positions of power use God's design of human creatures for their own self-satisfaction, the church must unequivocally condemn the abuse and protect the victims. But we must resist the temptation to imagine that all touch is bad as well. God has made us for physical touch.

Physicality isn't the problem; the perversion of abuse is the problem. Suitable child-protection policies and thoughtful accountability can and must help protect the community so that healthy and God-honoring practices can occur among the people of God. Instances of abuse are not only deviations from God's good gift of physical touch and care, but a rejection of God-given limits on us and of the dignity of the victim. Whether by cruel punches, violent words, or unwanted touches, the abuser is seizing power and control over another person who belongs only to God. By wickedly rejecting the divinely given good restraints of our holy Creator, abusers are not only hurting others; they're also deforming themselves. But just as our history of verbal abuse shouldn't push us to complete silence,

> [Jesus] touched her hand, and the fever left her.
>
> —Matthew 8:15

the proper response to physical abuse is not to rule out all contact. The only thoroughly realistic response here is to look to the one perfect man not only for answers but for life.

Jesus was so different. He did not hesitate to welcome, to touch, to greet others as if he belonged to them. The Gospels have good reason to highlight the fact that not just men but women also followed Jesus in the worst of times (e.g., Luke 23:27, 49). Women in first-century Judea were subject to cultural barriers and negative expectations, but the Gospels reflect Jesus's affirmative perspective toward his female contemporaries, who ended up being crucial for the early church. Rather than describing women generically or anonymously, the Gospels present us with women by name and with their different personalities. Mary, Joanna, and Susanna, for example, proved vital to Jesus's ministry (8:1–3). Likewise, certain women from Galilee observed how his body was laid in the tomb and then returned with burial spices to honor his dead body (23:55–24:1). *He honored their bodies, and they wanted to honor his.*

His presence—*his body*—was never a threat to women or children (Mark 9:33–37), nor did he dominate, manipulate, or abuse them. Instead, he loved them. His physical presence was a comfort. This reflects who he was and is.

Jesus fittingly loved well and honored physicality (even while displaying his lordship) when he bent the knee as a servant and took a towel and a basin of cool water to clean his disciples' feet, one at a time (John 13:4–5). The disciples' feet would have been exposed to the muck of first-century Palestinian roads, even if they had worn the usual sandals. The surface of the roads often consisted of a mixture of dust and excrement, both animal and human. Jesus's act would not have been like kissing the toes of a freshly washed infant; instead, his fingers went over heavily worn heels and misshapen toes, with bony knobs and abundant calluses.

We cannot disentangle our flesh from our souls or our minds from our bodies. Attempting to do so denies the reality of our wholeness as God has created us. It denies our finitude. Our bodies, with all their needs and dependencies, were made good. And our bodies need other bodies. Thankfully, the body of Christ is meant to be a sacred community in which holy healing takes place with dignity, honor, and love.

QUESTIONS FOR REFLECTION

- When have you felt seen and loved through healthy physical touch? Was that touch offered by a loved one? A friend? A spouse? Why was it so meaningful to you?
- How well do you think your church is helping to protect the vulnerable from various forms of physical abuse or mistreatment?
- How can you appropriately and compassionately follow Jesus's example in caring physically for your brothers and sisters? In what ways might properly loving your sisters and brothers cost you? How might Jesus's washing of his disciples' feet and his physical suffering and death for his enemies reshape your view of neighbor love?
- Why might the Gospel writers have consistently emphasized that Jesus touched people when he brought healing or a word of courage?

Identity beyond the Self

My own identity crucially depends on my dialogical relations with others.

—Charles Taylor, *Multiculturalism*

Despite our culture's calls to "be true to yourself" and "just be you," that same culture often interferes with our attempts to know who we are. Although these calls are worded in terms of liberation, they often produce far more restlessness and self-doubt than clarity. As we will see, we can and should value our particularity, viewing it in relation to our communities, culture, and history rather than in a disconnected way. So how do we go about knowing ourselves? Let's begin with what is undeniable but far too often ignored: you have a . . . belly button.

Just days away from leaving for Christmas break, I look out at the exhausted faces of my students. Many of them will soon head home. They can't wait to sleep! But experience tells me that going home is not necessarily a blessing for each of them. Often such trips mean returning to complicated family dynamics or even dysfunctional relationships. Students may love their parents, but that doesn't always make their relationship with them easy, and sometimes they're painfully difficult. Others head home with joy and expectation; since absence often does make the heart grow fonder (or at least forgetful!), and since they have fairly healthy relationships with their folks, they are filled with warm feelings of anticipation. And yet . . .

It doesn't take more than a few days, no matter the background, for the average young adult to become irritated with Dad—the way he breathes so loud or is incredibly awkward in public. Or maybe they become frustrated with Mom, whose questions were welcomed at first but now feel intrusive and tiresome. Whatever the reason, within a few days the college student returns to the struggle of relating to their parents.

Drawing from former Duke professors Stanley Hauerwas and William H. Willimon, I give my students a homework assignment over the break. It's a dangerous one. After being home for a bit, as the frustrations emerge and the distance between student and parent threatens to grow, I encourage them to . . . take a look at their belly button. Why? Because during these times of growing pains, it is all too easy in today's Western culture to imagine that we are self-made people. Hauerwas and Willimon, when exploring the biblical commandment to honor your parents, explain: "Nothing is quite as ontologically revealing as our belly button. . . . By noting that we are creatures, creations of mothers and fathers, the Decalogue tells us that

> You must necessarily come to the end of yourself (your false self!), and find that this is yet a beginning of a new life, . . . animated by God's abiding Spirit in you. Living from your core, where the Spirit dwells, you can relinquish the need to fix, to control, and to conquer, and drink in God's life, a life animated by peace, rest, wholeness, love, forgiveness, and surrender. It's the good life.
>
> —Chuck DeGroat, *Toughest People to Love: How to Understand, Lead, and Love the Difficult People in Your Life—Including Yourself* (Grand Rapids: Eerdmans, 2014), 160.

we have life as a gift. We are begotten, not manufactured. No wonder some of us despise our parents, for they are a visible, ever-present reminder that we were created, that the significance of our lives is not exclusively self-derived."[1]

The belly button, as Hauerwas and Willimon say, has profound theological importance. It's a bodily reminder that we are not self-made people. Instead, we are inevitably and necessarily bound together with others; it has been so from the beginning and will always be. Each of us is someone's child, whether we know their names or not. All of us owe our existence not simply to God but to other human creatures.

Once we start to ponder this reality, we realize that our whole lives, from our food to our shelter, from our health to our incomes—all of it involves the interdependence of human beings. Why? Because we are finite creatures. And the gift of these relationships with God, others, and even the earth provides the matrix for self-understanding, giving our lives meaning and purpose despite our social and economic statuses. Ironically, only when I stop thinking of myself as chiefly an isolated center of consciousness and consider my identity in terms of my relationships with others can I start to see clearly who I am.

QUESTIONS FOR REFLECTION

- What are the differences between considering ourselves as begotten versus self-made? What pressures push you toward a self-image that denies your relationships (with parents, neighbors, fellow churchgoers, etc.)?

- Whether we have wonderful or deeply hurtful relationships with our parents, we can all benefit from remembering that we are not "self-created." And we can sometimes even benefit from remembering that our parents also came from others. How might you express

gratitude anew to your parents? Or, have you considered cultivating compassion toward your parents as you
consider their own hurt, whether in their childhood or
other areas of life?

• Romans 12:4–13 and 1 Corinthians 12:4–31 discuss the
connectivity of Christians with Christ and each other.
Consider the image of a united body with diverse members. An eye and an ear don't perceive the world the
same way, and that difference can lead either to arguments and alienation or to a deeper understanding of
the world and the body of Christ. How do you evaluate
such possibilities in your relations with Jesus and those
around you?

The Self in Social Context

The strong concept of community means that the common good takes precedence over the individual good.

—Samuel Waje Kunhiyop, *African Christian Ethics*

Historically—and it is still true today in much of the non-Western world—the default way people viewed themselves (the "self") was *through their social relations*. Who am I? I am a daughter or son from this family who works in this trade and lives in this land. Identity was mostly found through social and physical locations and networks rather than through introspection. You looked outside yourself, rather than just inside. Questions of identity were less about solitary figures and far more about communities and connections. You defined who you were in terms of whose you were (your parents, clan, land, etc.). Some of the results were good (e.g., relationships connected people) and some were bad (e.g., sinful power structures often distorted and abused those relationships).

Negatively, this relational approach to selfhood could lose an individual in the crowd and its expectations, not able to develop any distinctive gifts. But God has not created humans as solitary creatures. From the beginning, "male and female he created them" (Gen. 1:27). This partnership of man and woman constitutes the first form of communion between persons. For by their innermost nature, human beings are social beings; if they do not affirm and participate with one another, they can neither live nor develop their gifts. We were made for community, but this is not to be confused with being forced into a mold of sameness.

Positively, when the relational dynamic of selfhood has functioned well, the burden of perceiving and defining one's identity has not been on the lone individual but shared among one's social connections. Each person has been able to find contentment by belonging to others and making contributions to the common good. By contrast, our strong tendency in the West to focus on our internal world alone can prevent us from realizing just how much (for good or ill) we are shaped by the social webs around us.

We are more a product of that which is outside us than inside us, and we cannot talk about what we love without referring to other people. In fact, most of what we experience "inside" ourselves—things deeply personal and private, both pleasurable and painful—is inseparable from relationships with others.

Consider such inner emotions as anger, sadness, or joy; these result from our *connections* to others and do not exist in some private, inner space untouched by the people around us. Worry, for example, often arises from fear of not measuring

The fellowship of the family is paramount in Proverbs, because we are just like malleable children and generally tend to adopt the personal characteristics and idiosyncrasies of those who are closest to us.

—Dominick S. Hernández, *Proverbs: Pathways to Wisdom*
(Nashville: Abingdon, 2020), 88.

up to perceived expectations of others important to us. Our worry about grades and academic achievement may feel self-imposed, but it frequently links back to childhood experiences that led us to believe our acceptance by others depended on our effort and performance. Does anxiety exist in any important way apart from pressures generated in the social arena? Not really.

If we fail to appreciate the social dynamics of our identity, we will too easily make the mistake of treating ourselves and others as isolated islands, not realizing how all of us are formed in communities and by subcultures. This happens when I *assume* my culture rather than relativize it, such as when I confuse my subculture's etiquette with binding biblical commands, asking others to conform to practices that make me comfortable but that really are not required for Christian faithfulness. All of us speak and act on the basis of our social locations and social histories, whether we acknowledge it or not.

While it is true that our identity is in Christ, that doesn't mean that our family, our culture, or other aspects of our particular experience are irrelevant. Our identity in Christ isn't something separate from our cultures and backgrounds; rather, it indicates how Christ transforms those other influences as he brings us to himself.

Sometimes our cultural assumptions make it hard to differentiate between sinful patterns and godly ones. For example, when does self-reliance transform from a positive virtue to arrogant isolation? This is part of why a healthy church, healthy family, and healthy friendships are vital to healthy spirituality. I need others if I am to be the most faithful version of "me." We expose one another's blind spots and help one another imagine a more beautiful, flourishing life. A significant Christian insight is that we flourish not by exalting ourselves but by learning to love and sacrifice for others as well as learning to accept such love and sacrifice from them.

QUESTIONS FOR REFLECTION

- Try to introduce yourself without making any references to groups that you associate with or are a member of. As sociologist Matt Vos points out, this exercise is harder than you might think, since almost everything—our languages, dietary preferences, clubs, and so on—has a social dimension.

- Now try introducing yourself again. Only this time, freely allow yourself to reference social groups. Talk about soccer teams, parents, spouses, partners, coworkers, and so on. How might this exercise help us better appreciate the social dimensions of self-understanding, especially in an age that imagines us as purely self-determined?

- Read 1 Corinthians 13 as a general exposition of how to love, and then read 1 Corinthians 16 as a set of instructions to the Corinthian church for loving the particular people around them in their own distinct circumstances. What's different from the rest of the world in these chapters? How does Jesus enable us to love in such a distinctive way from day to day?

Dietrich Bonhoeffer on Connection

We are and remain unknown to ourselves—known only by God.

—Dietrich Bonhoeffer, sermon on Luke 17:33

Addressing a small church of eighty people in Madrid, Spain, on October 21, 1928, a twenty-two-year-old German pastor named Dietrich Bonhoeffer (1906–45) preached a short sermon. On his mind were the struggles of the youth who were present; their wrestling with identity questions provided an opportunity for him to help the whole congregation think about a question that has particular force in modernity: "Who am I?" His text was Luke 17:33: "Whoever seeks to preserve his life will lose it, but whoever loses his life will keep it."

In this sermon, Bonhoeffer addressed the psychological mysteries people face when they begin to "become the object of their own observation." As they begin to ask about the "I" (the ego), they start to recognize that they are a "separate self" from others.[1] This process can be a painful, turbulent development, characterized by an internal "seething and surging and raging." The differences between how we perceive ourselves and how we think others perceive us can gain unsettling power. It is commonly understood that people—not just celebrities but also your coworkers and classmates—use social media platforms to construct public images of themselves that don't match reality.

Bonhoeffer's reflections on the "separate self" give us insight into that mismatch. He testifies that people bounce ideas around in their heads, unable to decide who they are: "That's me? No, that's not me. . . . It is me, for in me, too, things are seething and surging like that." In that turbulence, we occasionally come up to the surface for a gulp of air, asking, "Who am I? Why am I here? Where did I come from? What am I to do?"

The transition from childhood to adulthood often involves an intense version of this turmoil, as does a midlife crisis or end-of-life self-reflection. When people of any age—especially those between the ages of fifteen and thirty—struggle with these kinds of questions, they sometimes are met with a few typical suggestions. Bonhoeffer is aware of these suggestions and mentions two, recognizing the shortcomings of each.

First, we repeat the ancient Greek admonition "Know thyself." While this admonition, inscribed in the temple of Apollo at Delphi, has been repeated through the ages by philosophers and teachers, it has the following problem: Who really ever knows themselves? We change over time, we surprise ourselves by our thoughts or actions, and we occasionally even lie to ourselves. Bonhoeffer comments, "We are and remain unknown to ourselves—known only by God." No matter how excited you might be about the Enneagram, even our self-understanding is limited, and we must acknowledge that limit if we take our creaturely finitude seriously.

> We are constantly tempted, as Adam was at the beginning, to think that we are actually sufficient unto ourselves, that we have life in ourselves.
>
> —John Behr, *Becoming Human: Meditations on Christian Anthropology in Word and Image* (Crestwood, NY: St. Vladimir's Seminary Press, 2013), 43.

Second, when self-knowledge has proven insufficient, we are sometimes pointed toward "self-control" or "self-formation." Existentialist philosophers have said that we can mold ourselves into what we want to be. In Christian circles, as Bonhoeffer observes, this often sounds more like a call to focus on the "soul," giving all one's attention to the internal world. But our self-control and inward focus are as limited as our other faculties. We easily overestimate our discipline and underappreciate the social relations at work.

The temptation to give unrealistically simple answers to complex matters appears in the church as well as in the world. One consequence of this heavily internalized view of the self is that it can reduce sin to feelings and motivations, ignoring our connections with the external world and the resources we have in our friends and fellow Christians.

QUESTIONS FOR REFLECTION

- How do you navigate the gap in your life between how you present yourself to others and how you think of yourself? How do you imagine God thinks about this tension in you?

- How well would you say you know yourself? In what ways might it be helpful to admit that we can't perfectly know ourselves?

- We use the phrase "known by God" sometimes, but have you ever slowed down and really considered the idea that no one—not even you—knows you as well as God does? When you think about this, how do you imagine God thinking of you (given his exhaustive knowledge of you)? Is he stern? Disappointed? Delighted? Compassionate? Whatever comes to mind in this exercise, take some time to honestly reflect on what you imagine God thinks of you.

Disordered Loves
and the Truth about Us

> To go against self is the beginning of salvation.
>
> —Evagrius Ponticus

According to Augustine (354–430), love is not something we creatures generate but a divine activity we participate in because we live in the flow of God's love. Sadly, sin so distorts our experience that we now often imagine ourselves, rather than God, to be central. And making ourselves central distorts our experience of love and how we think about ourselves and others. One result of this fallen condition is that we now often live out our relationships in a self-centered way, as if we were the originators of love. As if love began and ended with us. But reconnecting with the God of love can help us to more fully experience not just divine love but neighbor love and even self-knowledge.

Consider how one's failure to know the concept or even the name of gravity doesn't reduce its presence and power. Similarly, ignoring the presence and power of divine love does not

> Authenticity is a harsh mistress for limited, doubled, and self-centered human beings. . . . It's like the difference between trying to smile and actually smiling. What's more, one can never be "authentic" enough; there's always someone more "real" than you.
>
> —David Zahl, *Low Anthropology: The Unlikely Key to a Gracious View of Others (and Yourself)* (Grand Rapids: Brazos, 2022), 157.

make it disappear. Our ignorance doesn't make it untrue! A right view of the self, then, always takes account of this web of relations with God, neighbor, and the rest of creation. Sadly, sin keeps bringing confusion, insecurity, and self-condemnation. Only God can restore us to our true selves and right relations, and only by resting secure in the divine benediction can we answer the question "Who am I?" Experiencing God's love opens up the world to us and allows for fuller self-knowledge, including further knowledge of (and comfort with) our finite particularity. Divine love alone can secure the one and the many, the whole and the part. Divine love holds us all together even when we fail to recognize it.

Self-knowledge is a good thing, but only God has perfect knowledge of anything, including ourselves. Still, our fellowship with God brings knowledge for the task at hand. This doesn't mean we can and will know everything, even about ourselves. But by entering the movement of God's love and action, we know ourselves more truly than endless self-examination could ever accomplish.

So who am I? I am a child of God who has been called to good and meaningful work. As a finite creature, I am from a particular place and people; I don't ignore my ethnicity, native language, socioeconomic setting, or relationships. As God's child, I am called not to deny my context or past but to see all of these realities transformed by God's holy love. His love shapes and reshapes my identity. Secure in Christ and aware of my dependence on others, I know that the Spirit works in me against the distorting effects of sin that harm the relationships God has created us for. I have been set free to undertake acts of love and reconciliation that build mutual, life-giving communion. This is the structure of my identity in Christ, in community, and in relation to the whole of God's creation.

QUESTIONS FOR REFLECTION

- What methods do you use to answer the question "Who am I?"
- How do you handle the paradox of setting your life aside to gain it? Can you think of any concrete examples that have made this paradox abundantly clear, either from your life or from the lives of others?
- Read John 15:1–11 and meditate on it as a pattern of love's action. If love requires work (as it does), how does this passage also reveal that our resting place is found in love?
- Have you ever considered God's intimate knowledge of you, paired with his deep love and grace toward you? How might soaking in this reality change how you view yourself and how you interact with others?

The Inner Conflict
of the Christian

As the gift of the new covenant, the Spirit makes real to (and in) believers "the truth as it is in Jesus." . . . What this means is that our selves are defined by and, indeed, *in* another. This is not simply formal but real, because of the Spirit's presence.

—Grant Macaskill, *Union with Christ in the New Testament*

A prisoner named Miguel, reflecting on suffering and related challenges, once said to me, "It's easy to make sense of lamenting to God when we're talking about people who haven't really done anything. We can understand their grief, their complaints, and their confusion before God amid their suffering and aches. But what about those who have done things, terrible things. Can they lament? And how should we view ourselves? My mom and my children are kept at arm's length even by the church because of what I did. So how am I to think about myself now?" Miguel had already been locked up for about fifteen years, the first ten in a very dangerous prison that was like hell. But even in a safer place, prison was still awful. Miguel is someone's son and another's father; a military veteran and former community member; a gentle, soft-spoken man; a murderer. So what is true about him? Who is he? Is he a man who wickedly killed another person? Yes. Is he a child of God who throws his entire hope on divine love and forgiveness? Yes. But what is *most* true about him? This isn't a debate about whether he should be in prison; it is a question about his identity. He now spends his time studying the Scriptures, in prayer, unevenly loving his neighbors within a rough context. Who is Miguel?

In the seventh chapter of his letter to some Roman Christians, the apostle Paul wrote of real internal conflict and confusion. "For I do not understand my own actions. For I do not do what I want, but I do the very thing I hate" (Rom. 7:15). Although scholars debate about how best to interpret this passage, we have good reason to think that when Paul speaks of this inner conflict, he is talking about not just people in general but Christians in particular. Although everyone experiences a psychological conflict like this, Christians experience it as a tension of living between what is often called the "now" (living in a fallen world) and the "not yet" (the freedom of glory we will one day experience). Our sin was crucified on the cross, so we are "saints" even now; yet our current experience often includes deep wrestling with ongoing sin and temptation.

Because Christ is the source of our life and being, the problem with our sin is less that we have broken a rule and more that we are not acting according to who we are. We properly respond to sin not by hating ourselves but by turning to Christ and trusting him, leaning on his Spirit to resist sin and to cultivate the

---

There is a great difference between those who put out the fire of sin within themselves by fear of hell or hope of future reward and those who from the feeling of divine love have a horror of sin itself.

—John Cassian, *Making Life a Prayer: Selected Writings of John Cassian*
(Nashville: Upper Room, 1997), 63.

fruit of love, joy, peace, patience, kindness, goodness, faithfulness, gentleness, and self-control.

Susan Eastman convincingly argues that Paul writes of Christian experience as a "double participation." Two things are true of believers living in this world: (1) Christ is victorious and we are secure in his finished work, and (2) since we still live vulnerably "in the flesh" this side of our own resurrection, we cannot escape ongoing challenges, either from within or from without.[1]

Although sin has disrupted all our relationships, God's breaking into time and space has accomplished what we could not do ourselves: he has brought us light, life, and reconciliation with himself. Given the conflicts around and within us, God alone can tell us what is most true about us. Yes, Miguel committed murder, but that is not what is most true about him. Actually, he is a saint, loved by God, forgiven, re-created, set free to love his (imprisoned) neighbors, and called to be an ambassador of reconciliation. This general truth is why Paul declares, "What we proclaim is *not ourselves*, but Jesus Christ as Lord, with *ourselves as your servants* for Jesus' sake" (2 Cor. 4:5).

QUESTIONS FOR REFLECTION

- How can the idea of giving ourselves away harmonize with the idea of truly being ourselves?
- Do you view anyone as beyond redemption? If so, how does this conflict with the content of today's meditation?
- How might viewing others as saints, loved by God, forgiven, re-created, set free to love their neighbors, and called to be an ambassador of reconciliation, change how you interact with them? In what ways might this mentality change the way you relate to yourself and others?
- Read 2 Corinthians 5:16–19. How radical is "new creation"? How does God reconcile us to himself in Christ? How does he reconcile us to one another in Christ?

Everything Points Back to Gift

The tree of life is high, and humility climbs it.
—Hyperichius

If you don't see your own finitude as a gift and a way of appreciating the gifts of others, then all you tend to see in others will be their problems and the ways they could be better. Of course, all people can "get better" at things. We can grow in our skill levels, develop stronger interpersonal abilities, or even acquire new skills. There is nothing wrong with that: much of Saint Paul's writing aims to encourage spiritual growth in his readers.

But the fool looks at others as isolated individuals and then wonders why they fall so short. This person is too detail focused and not relational enough, while that one is too relational and unable to accomplish goals. She loves vision but struggles with implementation; he loves the daily grind but seems unable to keep in mind larger goals and priorities. It's like the guy who endlessly dates different women—because he likes aspects of each of them, he keeps breaking up with them imagining he can find a single woman who has all of those characteristics. Looking at the problem like that, we see how ridiculous that

> Common benefits [we receive from God] are commonly slighted or not taken notice of. While the whole world shares with us the glorious and admirable benefit of light, we seldom consider what cause of thanksgiving we have for that mercy, and so for the air, fire, water, summer, winter, and the like.
>
> —Lucy Hutchinson, "On the Principles of the Christian Religion," in *The Works of Lucy Hutchinson*, ed. Elizabeth Clarke, David Norbrook, and Jane Stevenson (Oxford: Oxford University Press, 2018), 2:271–72.

attitude is in business or marriage, because we realize we are asking a single individual to have all the skills, all the experience, all the power and ability. We, not they, are the problem here, for we are trying to live a myth rather than a reality. Each person we meet is gifted, valuable, and beloved by God—and we are embedded in community with them.

True Christian humility does not simply bow down and worship God; it also elevates others and gives us an appropriate assessment of ourselves.

Ethicist Alasdair MacIntyre once observed, "Aristotle would certainly not have admired Jesus Christ and he would have been horrified by St. Paul."[1] Why? Because of their view of humility. To praise humility as a goal and a mode of living does not make sense in the conceptual world of this Greek philosopher.

We enter society by moving through the birth canal, right into a large web of mutual relations—moms and dads, doctors and nurses, teachers and farmers, sisters and brothers. We don't cause ourselves to have a brain, a will, affections, or a body—everything about our existence points back to *gift*. Yes, our existence results from the sexual union of a man and a woman, but even that physical union is part of a larger network of connections, with DNA and life stories, languages and traditions. Your belly button is your personal token of connection to your parents and the whole history of the human race.

And yet we occasionally hear it said, "He's a self-made man" and "No one helped me or gave me anything; I'm an independent person, needing no one." *Self-made*—really? No belly button? We experience a cultural pressure to be at least self-sufficient, if not exactly "self-made." We tend to admire the driven individual who seeks personal triumph more than we do the relational person who lives well-connected within a community.

We do well to extol this virtue of celebrating the abilities of others and seeing our life as a gift because we have derived it from a Judeo-Christian concept of the human person. Not everyone, however, holds to such a concept. In our culture, we confront competing views that derive from pagan philosophies like those of Aristotle or modern existentialists. Thus, we live in a tension between the current Western (largely pagan) focus on self-actualization and ancient Christian values and vision.

Christianity proclaims that humility is good and right, largely because it has an accurate assessment of ourselves and others. All we have is a gift from God, and others are part of that gift. We are not solitary or isolated figures but neighbors, living near one another, created for mutual reliance on one another, and we cannot exist without all that the earth provides for us. Biblical humility looks and sounds most like gratitude to God and neighbor.

QUESTIONS FOR REFLECTION

- When do you find yourself attempting to be ruggedly independent, and why do you think that is?
- How does your theology of humility change when you think of life as a gift instead of something you build from the ground up?
- How might this different view of humility, together with a view of finitude as gift, change how you interact with others? Would it allow you to show them more

grace and kindness? How might it change how you extend grace and kindness to yourself?

- In John 13:34–35, what is "new" about Jesus's command that his disciples love one another? Look at other
passages from previous meditations and ask how they
reflect this love.

Rethinking Humility

Humility is the self turned outward. . . . Humility is not thinking you are small. It is thinking that other people have greatness
within them.

—Rabbi Jonathan Sacks,
"The Greatness of Humility (Shoftim 5776)"

Christians have often grounded the need for humility in our *sin*.
Bernard of Clairvaux (1090–1153), who has some profoundly
helpful things to say about humility, nevertheless defines it thus:
"the virtue which enables a man to see himself in his true colors
and thereby to discover his *worthlessness*."[1] Some translate
Bernard's wording as "vileness" instead of "worthlessness,"
but both are very strong. Though in the same treatise Bernard
points to Christ as the model of humility, his definition raises
puzzling questions. Is Jesus humble because he is vile or worthless? Is the taking on of human flesh necessarily "vile"? That
description doesn't fit the portrayals in the New Testament, and
Bernard never adequately addresses the problem.

Theophilus, an early bishop of Alexandria (serving as patri-
arch from 385 to 412), went to Mount Nitria to meet a hermit
there and glean from his wisdom. Upon arriving, he asked the

> A politics of gratitude involves a modesty about the ability of the state to solve social problems, an economy that works at a human scale, emphasizes localism, and protects property rights instead of pursuing limitless growth. A politics of gratitude leads to environmental politics that respect the earth as a creation, to social policies that protect the family, to educational reforms that root students in their surroundings rather than detaching them from their surroundings.
>
> —Peter J. Leithart, *Gratitude: An Intellectual History*
> (Waco: Baylor University Press, 2014), 223.

hermit: "What have you discovered in your life, abba?" The ascetic declared, "To blame myself unceasingly."[2] While there is a nugget of truth in this expression, it confuses humility with self-loathing. They are not the same thing!

Here is a question well worth wrestling with: If humans had never sinned or experienced the fall, would we have any need for humility?

Put differently, is humility, as discussed in the Old and New Testaments, precisely a rejection of sin and no more? As serious as sin is, to treat it as the most important aspect of our existence and then to use it as the starting point for understanding what it means to be human contradicts God and the goodness of creation. Any building on such a foundation is compromised. The results are often ugly, destructive, and unstable.

Ugly versions of humility have popped up through the ages (e.g., self-harm and a constant belittling of oneself), built on a foundation that could never inform us truly about God's good creation. In short, taking sin as our starting point for a doctrine of humility twists our understanding and hurts us.

Instead of starting with sin, we must ground our theology of humility in the goodness of *creation*. Humility is a distinctly biblical virtue because *it begins with the knowledge that a good creator Lord exists and that we are the finite creatures he has made to live in fellowship with him.* Everything—from the air we breathe to the water we drink, from our eyes to our taste buds—goes back to this gift of blessed existence. Our being itself comes out of the overflow of divine love and creativity.

Humility consists in a recognition of (and a rejoicing in) the good limitations that God has given us; humility is *not* a regrettable necessity, nor simply a later addition responding to sinful disorders. Humility is the path of freedom and joy. Even if humans had never fallen into sin, humility would still have the essential character of gratitude for our dependence on God and for his faithful supply of our needs. Humility is built on the Creator-creature distinction and connection; its response to sin emphasizes our further need for God to restore us to the fellowship that he has always intended us to inhabit.

What difference does our reason for humility make? Building on creation rather than sin avoids distortions like un-Christian self-hatred ("I'm so terrible I'm not worth anything") and self-absorption ("Look at me; I'm humble!"). While our struggles with sin and its distortion of our lives can, of course, reinforce the need for humility before God, his acts of creation and redemption alone (not our sin) are the solid foundation on which we can build our doctrine and experience.

QUESTIONS FOR REFLECTION

- In your view, is it problematic to build a doctrine of humility on sin? Why or why not? And if so, how is it problematic?
- In what ways might Adam and Eve have demonstrated humility?
- How might recognizing the "greatness in others" relate to the practice of humility? Does it make you

uncomfortable to see greatness in others? If so, consider why that might be the case.

- In Matthew 11:28–29, how does the fact that Jesus is "lowly in heart" recommend him to those who are weary and burdened?

DAY 20

Humility in Worship and Love of Neighbor

Between the being of God and that of man remains the gulf of creaturehood, and creaturehood means precisely this: the being of each human person is given to him.

—John Zizioulas, *Being as Communion*

Thomas Aquinas (1225–74) discusses humility with care and therefore deserves our attention. He advocates humility as "a praiseworthy self-abasement to the lowest place."[1] "Self-abasement" could indicate a belittling of oneself or even a movement toward self-hatred, but a fuller reading of Aquinas will interpret this word choice as focusing on the good of others rather than on one's own need. Aquinas links self-abasement to being a dependent creature, and he later notes that the language of humility comes from *humo acclinis*, which literally means "bent toward the ground." Such an etymology points to an awareness of and connection with the "dust and ashes" motif of Scripture (see, e.g., Gen. 18:27).

Unlike Aristotle, Aquinas distinguishes between magnanimity, the "stretching forth of the soul to great things," and pride, which aims "at greater things through confiding in one's own powers," rather than "through confidence in God's help, which is not contrary to humility."[2] Simply put, pride ignores God as the giver of one's mind and skills, whereas humility gratefully employs these gifts as an expression of worship and as a way to help others. G. K. Chesterton compares Aristotle's magnanimous man, "who is great and knows that he is great," with Aquinas's view of the "miracle of the more magnanimous man, who is great and knows that he is small."[3]

Humility and magnanimity are, as Mary Keys explains, twin virtues (*duplex virtus*) that should belong together when we consider "greatness" and the use of one's gifts.[4] No matter how "great" one is, all one's actions ought to be (and, apart from the fall, could be and would have been) expressions of worship of God and in generous service of neighbor. Jesus kneeling down and washing the dusty feet of his disciples is, for Aquinas, the model of the humility we ought to imitate.

Aquinas believes that faintheartedness can, just like arrogance, grow out of pride: "A man clings too much to his own opinion, whereby he thinks himself incompetent for those things for which he is competent."[5] Other people are good at helping us discover not only our faults but also our gifts. It would be foolish to imagine any of us has all possible gifts, and it would be equally arrogant to neglect celebrating the gifts God has given to others. The goal of humility, then, is love! Love is how God animated the world in the first place.

Augustine identifies the humility of Jesus with Jesus's *glad dependence* on the Father.

—Kent Dunnington, *Humility, Pride, and Christian Virtue Theory*, Oxford Studies in Analytic Theology (Oxford: Oxford University Press, 2018), 41.

To know what you really think of God and your relationship with him, watch how you respond to your neighbor. If we don't love our neighbor, then chances are pretty good that we don't love God either (1 John 4:21).

Humility opposes sin just as sin opposes humility. Humility, as a pattern of life and love with God and neighbor, is a tool that helps us fight and avoid sin. God calls us to humility not so that he might feel better about himself but in order that his goodness might again be made manifest in worship, neighbor love, and the stewardship of the earth. Humility both rests on and points back to the goodness of creation, and it points forward to the promise of new creation.

QUESTIONS FOR REFLECTION

- How have you seen humility and praise of others conflict in the past? Have you felt the tension between these two? Why do you think this tension exists?

- Have you thought about humility as worship of God or as a self-conjured virtue? How does Aquinas's idea of humility as "confidence in God's help" change your thinking?

- Read Philippians 2:3. If selfishness and empty conceit hide the truth from us, how do humility and "count[ing] others more significant than yourselves" reveal the truth?

Cultivating Humility

For, what pride can be cured, if it is not cured by the humility
of the Son of God?

—Augustine, *The Christian Combat*

The Son of God did not consider equality with God a thing
to be grasped, but made himself nothing, taking the form of
a servant (Phil. 2:6–7). We identify with those in misery for at
least three reasons: First, that's exactly what God in Christ has
done and continues to do. Second, the only life we live now is
life in Christ. To participate in his life requires us to participate
in his work, and that participation means ministering to the
weak, the vulnerable, the hurting, and the sinner. Third, when
we do so, we find ourselves at home.

Do you want to know where God's heart goes out to? Follow
the weakness, follow the need, follow the cries. How do you
"cleanse your hands" and "purify your hearts" (James 4:8)?
Become friends with the wounded and needy (cf. Rom. 12:16).
In the New Testament letter of James, after calling his readers
to be particularly mindful of orphans and widows (1:27), the
author calls his readers to grieve, mourn, and wail (4:8–10).

Arrogance is as ugly as humility is beautiful.

—John Dickson, *Humilitas: A Lost Key to Life, Love, and Leadership* (Grand Rapids: Zondervan, 2011), 82.

Sounding like the prophet Isaiah (e.g., Isa. 1:11–17), James here is calling us to be aware of the misery of others in the world, including the poor and those with no family or social resources. Their tears become our tears; their fears and pain cause us to wail; their hurt is our hurt. We stand not as outsiders but as their friends. In this way, we find ourselves concerned about injustice, drawn to the orphan and the widow, and sensitive to the marginalized. James is unflinching when he calls us to stop flirting with the adulterous powers and dominions of the world and to start reflecting the humility of God's Son. Christ, the embodiment of humility, lifts others up that they might see God. The only one who has the right to judge is the truly humble one, yet he proclaims grace on those who judged him (Luke 23:34).

Now let's return to grounding our call to humility in the goodness of creation.

Humility does not simply say, "I'm sorry" or "Please forgive me." Humility also says, "I don't know," "Can you help me?" and "How should I do this?" It begins by saying, "God favors me, so I don't have to be self-absorbed," "Loving people is the most sensible way to live," and "I can't do everything, but God reigns and cares for me and others, so that's okay." Humility is not chiefly a response to sinful behaviors, because it has taken to heart our situation as finite creatures and appreciates the goodness of mutual dependence and love.

Humility opposes the pride and hubris of sin, as well as the fear and desperation of sin. Consequently, the humble not only recognize their limits before God and neighbor, but they also ask for forgiveness when they have wronged others.

Our limits are no longer seen as a threat. We don't have to grab every commodity we can store, nor must we figure everything out. Yes, we should work, learn, and most importantly love, but this will all be motivated by the peace of humility rather than frantic self-centeredness. We are not self-made, self-kept, or self-saved.

Unfortunately, we are not merely finite creatures but also rebellious sinners. Humility equips us to repent of rebelling against God and harming our neighbors and the earth. Humility is our stance of openness toward our Creator and Redeemer, our preparation for worship, delight, and love. Humility equips us to better understand our place in the world, allowing us to become more patient and less anxious, which is an ongoing challenge.

QUESTIONS FOR REFLECTION

- How does an understanding of humility as focusing on others harmonize with the idea that humility also involves asking for help?
- What does it mean for you to think of humility as preparation? As openness?
- Read Philippians 4. Notice how this chapter combines instructions for serving one another with instructions for looking to the Lord for help.
- Paul defines two elements of humility before he upholds Christ as the supreme example in Philippians 2:3–4: giving honor and empathizing. How might we cultivate these two characteristics in ourselves, our families, and our communities? Consider how different this approach is from common strategies that seek to grow humility primarily through self-criticism.

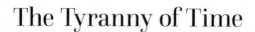

The Tyranny of Time

God never changes.
Patience attains
All that it strives for.
He who has God
Finds he lacks nothing:
God alone suffices.
　　　　—Teresa of Ávila,
　　　　　　"Poem IX"

Augustine once quipped, "What then is time? Provided that no one asks me, I know."[1] Looking at my watch, I tell you the time, and while scholars call this "clock time," people have not always experienced time this way. Really, then, what is this thing called "time"?

In a sense, telling time is nothing new, but people have experienced time much differently from clock time. People have used the sun, the stars, and the moon as their temporal scales for millennia. The book of Genesis represents an ancient ordering around the sun and the moon that "separate[d] the day from the night" (1:14). As acclaimed scholar Roland de Vaux once explained, though many people later counted each "day" from evening to evening, early on Israel counted a "day" from morning to morning and followed natural patterns to divide the day into times of morning, midday, and dusk. Israel also attended to time by marking the breeze before sunrise, the hottest time of the day, the evening breeze, and the setting of the sun. Embodiment in the material world shaped our relation to time: what we saw, experienced, and felt governed this sense of moving through each day.

Scholars call it "contextual time" when we draw from nature to create temporal references. Thus, some days are "longer" than others, some seasons are more appropriate for harvest or festivals and feasts, and some hours are more fitting for napping than labor. Childbirth brings expectations that differ from those associated with war. Before the arrival of mechanized clocks and then electricity, time was not an abstract idea or a detached aspect of the world; it *necessarily* related to one's physical environment, community dynamics, and the rhythms of the created world. However, with the arrival of such clocks and electricity, we moved from contextual to noncontextual time, which deeply reshaped our expectations of time.

We must . . . assert a fundamental link between human life and the life of God. . . . These times must include not only a limited set of special times—the Sabbath, say, or only acts of devotion or holiness—but all times, of every kind. Most importantly for our self-understanding as creatures, God's time includes the times that mark our coming to be, our survival, and our passing away: times of birth, growth, eating, learning, sexual engagement, relating, work, birthing, forming, weakening, and dying.

—Ephraim Radner, *A Time to Keep: Theology, Mortality, and the Shape of Human Life* (Waco: Baylor University Press, 2016), 8.

The development of Christian time is an increasingly detailed affirmation of how the structure of history, and of the cosmos in and through which history flowed, reveals and serves God and calls humans to God's service.

—Andrew B. McGowan, *Ancient Christian Worship: Early Church Practices in Social, Historical, and Theological Perspective* (Grand Rapids: Baker Academic, 2014), 218.

Centuries ago, Christian monasteries, following Benedict's *Rule*, began to use clocks to structure each day for worship. Bells rang to announce the hours of the Divine Office—the repeated pattern of praise and worship at different hours of the day. However, liturgy, rather than some abstract sense of time limits, guided this daily structure, with the sounds of chiming simply helping participants move back and forth between prayer and work.

But clocks did not stay in monasteries or town squares alone. As they became more common and eventually occupied homes, they began to change the human experience of time at large. Eventually, clocks displayed not just hours but minutes and seconds, one after another, never ending, always pushing us forward.

Judy Wajcman, in her book *Pressed for Time: The Acceleration of Life in Digital Capitalism*, reminds us that "qualities such as speed and efficiency are not produced by technologies alone but are related to social norms that evolve as devices are integrated into daily life."[2] For example, smartphones and laptops help improve life outcomes by giving us greater flexibility at work and better long-distance communication, but they have also eroded the boundaries between employment and leisure, between school and home, between day and night. Being "on the clock" has been replaced by never leaving it! As we flip on the kitchen lights and awaken the computer, it doesn't matter if it's dark outside, if our bodies feel exhausted, if our child is sick, or if our blood sugar is low—all that matters is that we have work to do and time to do it. In clock time, an hour is an hour, whether it starts at 11 a.m. or 11 p.m. Modern technology— including everything from electricity to home Wi-Fi—has now totally *decontextualized* time, detaching it from our bodies and our environments. Can you feel it?

Generally speaking, the problem is that we have changed our expectations and how we relate to time. This has resulted in trying to do more than we ever used to. By "more," I mean not only more paid work but more activities in all the other areas of life (more kids' sports, more meetings, more entertainment, more exercise, more . . .).

What we really want is to live in harmony with time, rather than to be driven by it. Irish poet and priest John O'Donohue once wrote that "stress is a perverted relationship to time."[3] He explains that when we are stressed, we no longer participate in time as we live in God's presence; instead, we are driven and pushed and eventually emptied by time.

Amid the busyness and endless movement of the clock, we feel we never have enough time. And one of the greatest costs of this state of affairs is that we start to find it more and more difficult to be fully present with God and others. But God is the ultimate "context" of our lives and of our time. Growing in our awareness of God's presence can reframe our temporal experience. We will return to this idea in the coming reflections.

QUESTIONS FOR REFLECTION

- Read Genesis 1:1–2:3. Does this different framework for time (from clock time to relational time) make you read it any differently? Instead of fitting the actions of this creation account into a clock-and-calendar scheme, think of them as generating the time and space for

God to enter into fellowship with his created world. The actions of days one through five have the creation of humans as their goal, but the absence of the latter doesn't empty the first five days of joy and beauty. Indeed, these days are full of goodness, according to God's comments.

- How have you seen your relationship with time affect your relationship with God? How might appreciating time in terms of events and contexts rather than merely the clock reshape our experiences? What might we learn from other cultures in this regard?

- What would it mean for you, as a Christian, to relate in a healthier way to time? How would that healthier relationship change your days? Your weeks? Your months? Your years?

Reconsidering Stress

A Friend Turned into an Enemy?

So teach us to number our days that we may get a heart of wisdom.

—Psalm 90:12

Although "stress" is a negative buzzword in our day, stress is not intrinsically bad. Girders on a bridge undergo stress as tension, pressure, and torsion (twisting). Stress is also a positive factor in human growth and development: bodies need appropriate levels of physical stress in order to grow properly; minds need to conquer new problems in order to learn. Looking at it in this way, we can view stress as an objective situation and view anxiety as one possible subjective response to it. High stress can break a girder or a body or a mind, but only the mind can be anxious about it.

In addition to provoking physical or mental growth, stress experienced as a psychological reaction to our circumstances can tell us that we have things to do and it's time to do them. No more putting them off. In this way, stress can be a genuinely

> The reason time feels like such a struggle is that we're constantly attempting to master it—to lever ourselves into a position of dominance and control over our unfolding lives so that we might finally feel safe and secure, and no longer so vulnerable to events.
>
> —Oliver Burkeman, *Four Thousand Weeks: Time Management for Mortals* (New York: Farrar, Straus & Giroux, 2021), 215.

good thing. It's noteworthy that the Bible never commands us, "Do not stress."

Your ability to react to stress is a gift from God. Your body senses a problem and decides to respond, sometimes with fight and other times with flight, either confronting or avoiding the threat. This capacity can be helpful not just in war or when walking alone at night but also when you're a student or a parent with lots to do. Stress can make you run faster and work harder. God made us as creatures who can appropriately respond to stress and thus save lives, get great things done, and react appropriately to serious needs.

But we have taken a good gift and made it a terrible master. We have accumulated stresses beyond our ability to bear them, plunging ourselves into constant anxiety. It's as if every day were harvest day, so every day is filled with extreme levels of stress. Rather than making it an occasional help, we've made stress a way of life. Yet God didn't design us for that.

We were never made to live on high alert *all* the time. We now commonly live with constant low-level stress from a mix of unrelenting demands, expectations, and endless distractions. A tweet from the president raises our blood pressure; a work email at 10 p.m. stirs the acids in our stomachs; pushing ourselves all weekend for kids' travel teams increases anxiety about returning to work on Monday.

Stress can be helpful as long as it is realistic, episodic, and addressed, as with a farmer working extra-long harvest days.

Stress often produces unhealthy forms of anxiety when we allow it to overload our capacity to handle it. Anxiety, when experienced as our negative response to the fact of stress, often changes us mentally, physically, and emotionally, reducing our ability to handle stress, thus making itself a bigger and bigger problem. In this situation, we often feel an emotional response telling us *we are not enough*. If God comes to mind, this form of anxiety tells us either that God is not enough or that he doesn't care. Such intense stress and growing anxiety tend to isolate and hurt us.

Our jobs and families involve hard work, and sometimes that means that we need to be stretched and work long hours. Clearly, some seasons and days require long hours, but we simply cannot sustain being on high alert all the time.

Both crunch time and periods of stillness and quiet can produce anxiety. Jumping among these extremes and all the situations between is unsettling, and we need to learn how to respond in a way that generates peace. We need to learn how to be present in each moment and not combine the stress of all our moments all the time. Presence requires us to face our limits, to learn to be where we are, and to recognize that we are not in control and not everything is up to us.

To be truly present has perhaps never been easy, but in our day, that difficulty seems only to have intensified. To be *here* doing *this* and not *somewhere else* doing *that* is surprisingly tough. To give full attention to the person standing in front of you, to be wholly present during the family meal, to enjoy rubbing your hands across the fur of your Labradoodle as you snuggle on the sofa—these are examples of being genuinely present in the moment, in real time and space. Such attention honors our limited presence and allows us to become more aware of God's presence. It also helps us learn how to be more realistic with our time, with our limited energy and attention.

Learning to be fully present takes practice in our context of clock time and technological advances. Tomorrow we will see how we need to make our presence a habit, a way of life.

QUESTIONS FOR REFLECTION

- How do you speak about and experience stress? What two to four things immediately come to mind as the major stressors in your life? Is there anything you could change to make these stressors more realistic, episodic, and addressable?

- How do you think of anxiety in relation to being present? How do you see these two concepts interacting in your own life?

- How would you describe the feeling of being fully present with God or others?

- Read Matthew 6:25–34. Does this teaching from Jesus look completely impossible to you? How would trusting God for tomorrow change today for you?

Divine Presence

We come into the presence of Christ to offer him our time, we extend our arms to receive him. And he fills this time with himself, he heals it and makes it—again and again—the time of salvation.

—Alexander Schmemann, *For the Life of the World*

If we are ever going to respond to the challenge of time, stress, and anxiety in a healthy Christian way, we don't just need better time management; we need to rediscover the fear of the Lord. That is, we need to become attentive to God's presence and provision.

Orthodox priest Alexander Schmemann points out that human beings have been made to live in communion with the triune God. He argues that the "secular" age posits the opposite, not so much by denying God's existence as by denying his presence, not denying the possibility of worship but its centrality.[1] We can even secularize our practice of Christianity.

Christians have often, without realizing it, fallen into secularism, not because we use electricity or buy iPhones but because we have confined worship to a single experience. Worship

In order to participate in God, we must acquire a divine sense. Such a sense involves love. The more we love, the more we receive and the greater is our participation in the God who is unseen.

—Christopher R. J. Holmes, *A Theology of the Christian Life: Imitating and Participating in God* (Grand Rapids: Baker Academic, 2021), 65.

for many people designates an hour or two a week, and even that is probably too generous. Often when you ask Christians about church, they might say, "I enjoyed the worship, but the preaching was bad, and the offering made me uncomfortable." "Worship" here doesn't even represent the whole Christian service; rather, it's reduced to the times of *singing* during that service. Maybe this reduction is because singing engages us in more holistic ways (i.e., mind, affections, body), that it can help us—even if only for a few moments—to focus more fully on God's reality, on his presence. But after those few minutes of singing are over, we go back to the rest of our secular lives, even as we still sit in the pews.

As this pattern and habit have set in, our world has become "disenchanted" to us. We no longer see and recognize God all around us. We live the majority of our time passively assuming God's absence rather than his presence—not because he isn't there, but because we're not attuned to his presence. We have disenchanted the world by emptying it of God, as it were, making it flattened and depersonalized. Even Christians often live such secular lives.

So how do we resist the suffocating effects of secularism? Worship! Schmemann comments, "Thus the very notion of worship is based on an intuition and experience of the world as an 'epiphany' of God, thus the world—in worship—is revealed in its true nature and vocation as 'sacrament.'"[2] Even if we don't affirm Schmemann's full sacramental view of the world, I do believe he points us in the right direction. Corporate worship gatherings can—in their entirety, from invocation to benediction (or from welcome to sending)—provide the clearest unveiling of God's presence and action in the world. But this unveiling is meant to illuminate the rest of our lives, not to contradict or fragment them.

The Wisdom literature of Israel repeatedly links the "fear of the LORD" with the "beginning of wisdom" (e.g., Ps. 111:10; Prov. 9:10; cf. Job 28:28). Such wisdom is the opposite of a secular perspective. In fact, the Wisdom literature often contrasts two ways of life: the way of the wise and the way of the fool (Prov. 1:7; cf. Ps. 1). What's the difference? It's not how well you do on a math quiz or how high your IQ is. No, what fundamentally distinguishes the wise from the foolish is that the latter either deny or ignore God (Pss. 14:1; 92:5–6), whereas the former live with an active sense of God's holy presence, good power, and wise provision, aware of God's love, forgiveness, and faithfulness. "The fear of the LORD is a fountain of life" (Prov. 14:27).

Living in the fear of the Lord is not so much about being scared (although sometimes that is an appropriate response, as in Ps. 76:7–12) as it is about recognizing God's real presence all around us, from our rising to our lying down, from our food to our sexual encounters, from our laughter to our intellectual burdens. As Hebrew Bible scholar Bruce Waltke has argued, biblical fear of the Lord operates at both the rational and nonrational levels, holding together both otherness and intimacy, both awe and love, both reverence and trust. Whereas pagan gods could be unpredictable, ambiguous, and manipulated, Yahweh was never unconcerned or exploited but always reliably good and holy, loving and wise. In a word, he was *present*!

As we navigate our stressful and anxious lives, we are invited to return to the fear of the Lord, to welcome God's presence and recognize his provision again. As we become more responsive to his presence, we also often become more present with our neighbors.

QUESTIONS FOR REFLECTION

- Compare David's and Saul's attitudes toward God in 1 Samuel 17:20–54. What assumptions about the presence and activity of God lie behind each attitude?

- Which aspect of corporate worship makes you feel the most present—singing, the preaching of the Word, the sacraments, or something else? Why?

- Where do you feel God is most present and most absent in your life? Why do you think that is? What might it look like to cultivate the fear of the Lord as you grow in your awareness of his presence?

The Fear of the Lord

God's time is created, gifted, slow, generous, gentle, and designed to enhance the purposes of love.

—John Swinton, *Becoming Friends of Time*

The fear of the Lord requires our full and authentic presence, which is why the Bible gives us a variety of ways to approach him according to our circumstances. From the praise that arises out of delight to the laments we cry in times of pain, God has taught his people to give voice to their lives before him, confident that he is listening and aware. He creates space not only for positive expressions of thanks but also for arguments, questions, frustrations, and distress (e.g., Exod. 32:1–14; Josh. 7:7; Ruth 1:21). All of these can be expressions of worship.

If God is ever-present, then he sees and knows everything; therefore, we go to him not with clichés or prepackaged answers but to wrestle and rest, to cry and laugh, to lay out our concerns even as we discover hope. And we do so not merely at a single time in the day but throughout the whole. Those who experience the fear of the Lord discover that praying without ceasing doesn't require that we enter a monastery; instead, it requires a mindfulness of God's presence. Such mindfulness fosters the

> That practice which is alike the most holy, the most general, and the
> most needful in the spiritual life is *the practice of the Presence of* GOD.
> It is *the schooling of the soul to find its joy in His Divine Companionship.*
>
> —Brother Lawrence, *The Practice of the Presence of God with Spiritual Maxims*
> (Grand Rapids: Spire, 1967), 70.

fear of the Lord. Writing in the twelfth century, Peter Lombard (1100–1160) reflected the tradition of linking this particular fear with being loved as part of God's family: "Filial fear now makes us fear *lest we offend the one whom we love* and lest we become separated from him."[1] This is not so much a fear of punishment as it is a fear of ignoring or insulting the one we love and the one who loves us. Jesus perfectly lived in the fear of the Lord because, by the Spirit, he saw everything in light of the presence and activity of his Father.

Fear and comfort, awe and love, presence and care all belong together. For Christians, this alone is the way to encourage a re-enchantment of this world—that is, to see it as inhabited by God.

By fearing the Lord, we can resist fearing our situations and circumstances. His presence informs and reforms our stories and our understanding of them. Strangely, when we lose our fear of the Lord, we also lose some perception of his comfort, love, and compassion, for in downplaying the otherness and nearness of God, we replace him—his *presence*—with ideas about him or with things that are clearly not God. And this replacement always ultimately leaves us wanting.

We seek distractions to avoid our weariness, to numb our sense of meaninglessness, or to fill the silence that haunts us. We try to derive self-understanding, values, and a sense of worth and direction from the creation instead of the Creator, who alone can show us these things.

This situation presents at least two dangers, one for material-ists and another for spiritualists. Materialists seek to ease the hectic pace and anxiety of life by distracting themselves with stuff and pleasure, but this doesn't work. Spiritualists seek to ease the pain and problems of life by disconnecting from the earth and relationships, imagining that to experience God's presence, we need an absence of materiality. But that doesn't work either.

Contrasting with these two mistakes, the fear of the Lord allows us to see God in and through everything without trying to make everything God. Rather than acting like a fool who thinks that God is absent or ignorant (Pss. 14:1; 53:1; cf. Prov. 14:7–9), the wise are led by the fear of God to recognize his presence and care. This fear shows divine mercies to the believer in unexpected places, supplies courage to do difficult things, reveals the beauty around us to be from the Lord, and strengthens us to fight against evil for justice and love. The fear of the Lord is not a flight from this world, but the only way of fully living in it *coram Deo*, before the face of God.

QUESTIONS FOR REFLECTION

- Do you consider yourself more a materialist or a spiritualist, as discussed in this chapter? Do you find all your meaning from material pleasures with little awareness of God's presence? Or do you seek forms of escapism that downplay God-given realities in your life (e.g., your relationships, physical body, job, etc.)? However you navigate these things, how might cultivating an awareness of God's presence make a difference?
- How have you thought about the phrase "the fear of the LORD"? How do you react to hearing this phrase in harmony with the words "comfort" and "love"?
- Read Psalm 34:7–10. What is the function and nature of the fear of God in this passage?

Process Matters

The new creature's response to the Spirit's work in and through him or her may be portrayed as a joyful yielding to the hands of the sculpting Spirit.

—Leopoldo A. Sánchez M., *Sculptor Spirit*

Many of us have difficulty valuing process. Our culture of rapid download speeds and instant gratification has little tolerance for tedious practices, the significance of slow growth, and the beauty of development.

With similar impatience, we often wonder why God doesn't just instantly change us. Sin is a present and continuing struggle for believers. Life dedicated to God takes great effort and perseverance. So we ask: When God extends his grace to our broken and needy lives, why doesn't he just immediately free us from our faults? Why are our bad habits not erased and positive virtues not instantaneously produced? If God doesn't like certain sinful attitudes and behaviors, why does it sometimes seem like he stops with forgiving us? Why doesn't the Almighty also instantly transform us so we never fall short again?

Christians often deal with a lot of guilt and shame because of their continued struggle with disobedience and sin. We also struggle with guilt and shame over our creaturely limits, which can manifest in everything from failing to remember Scripture to falling asleep while praying. We can feel that we should know more, do more, be more. Always more. Seeing how far short we fall from a finished product weighs on us. In response, we ask whether God is in fact constantly frustrated or angry with us. Is he persistently irritated with his children, or is something else going on? Might it be true that though he clearly does not enjoy our sin, he values the process of our growth and the work involved in it, not just the final product?

When my kids were learning to walk, I would stand them up so they could hold the side of the couch with one hand. Backing away about eight feet, I would then call them, grinning widely and making hand gestures to encourage them in my direction. Eventually, their courage stirred them to take that first step, removing their hands from what they previously rested on. Inevitably, they wouldn't make it very far—maybe a foot or two. Then they would fall. Sometimes they would cry; other times they might just hit the ground and look up, wondering how I would respond. Do you think that when they fell, I immediately shouted at them, "You idiots, what are you doing? I clearly told you to walk"? Of course I didn't say that. What loving parent would? But did you just feel a physical reaction when reading those incendiary words? How cruel they were. How irrational. No, when my children fell, I would immediately rush over to

By learning their part in [Scripture's] story, Christians claim to have a narrative that can provide the basis for a self appropriate to the unresolved, and often tragic, conflicts of this existence.

—Stanley Hauerwas, *A Community of Character: Toward a Constructive Christian Social Ethic* (Notre Dame, IN: University of Notre Dame Press, 1981), 149.

them, lift them up, offer fresh assurances and love, and then set them up to try again. I was kind and compassionate, not because I was indifferent to their learning to walk but because I understood their situation. I knew where they were and where they needed to be, but I was also fully aware of the genuine challenge. Learning to walk is necessarily a process, one that requires repeated effort.

Why do we pit compassion against success, grace against growth, and tenderness against effort? I delighted to see my children grow, to observe them developing new skills and competencies, even when doing so meant a lot of crashing onto the floor.

By contrast, we often think very poorly of our heavenly Father in similar situations, though we would never admit it. We seem to believe that he expects us to be instantly flawless, never making a mistake, never falling back or hitting the ground. When we do fall, we suspect that he is surprised and frustrated—as if the holy, omniscient God were naive or ignorant about the ways sin has so deeply affected us or the ways he himself has created us with good limitations. Subconsciously, we suppose that because we are Christians, our thoughts, words, and actions should be instantly free from ever lapsing into sin and failure again.

When we assume that God is temperamental, the Christian life seems heavy and burdensome rather than hopeful and promising. We endure rather than enjoy it. But if we better understood our God, who abounds with compassion and grace, we might more freely grow in our Christian lives without being crushed by our weaknesses and limits.

Far too often, we have tried to make sense of Christian spirituality and sanctification while forgetting that our limitations are included in God's original blueprint, that his tenderness toward us is only increased by our deep need for him, and that sin hasn't removed any of that. Neglecting our background distorts our view of the Christian life, producing timidity instead of confidence, fear instead of hope, and a sense of exhaustion and exile instead of welcome and rest. But the Spirit of creation is the same as the Spirit of sanctification, and therefore God is working in us over the whole of our lives, not just at the moment of our conversion. He values process and not just finished products.

QUESTIONS FOR REFLECTION

- How do you approach the fact that God values process as he transforms you to more and more reflect Christ? Does this process often frustrate you? How does it affect your prayer life?

- Do your limits make you feel stunted? If so, how can you incorporate this struggle into your requests before God?

- Read Isaiah 40:1–11. Notice the gentleness with which God leads his flock in this passage, concerned as he is for the weakness and fragility of each particular sheep. How does this fit with your understanding of God's attitude toward you?

DAY
27

Valuing Design

Is God Efficient?

The artist is nothing without the gift, but the gift is nothing without work.

—Émile Zola

Church buildings can be designed in different styles. Accordingly, a community expresses its values in its architecture. With that in mind, some ask, "Shouldn't a church be as basic as possible, with the cheapest construction allowable so that all the extra money can go directly to missions and helping the poor? Why would you ever pay to have higher ceilings than necessary? Why spend energy and resources on landscaping—won't asphalt and concrete cover the ground just as well? Wouldn't nonessential architectural 'extras' be a form of self-indulgence?" Maybe. The definition of "indulgent" is "having or indicating a tendency to be overly generous to or lenient with someone."[1] Is God too generous with the design of his creation? With us? Must we understand indulgence in a negative way? Maybe "indulgent" isn't a good word for describing God, but I do want us to reconsider how we imagine God and his view of his creation, including us.

Historians of architecture and social critics have long observed that the construction of buildings, especially housing, only on the basis of mechanical and financial efficiency has significant negative consequences. Ugly community housing can suck the morale out of those who live there. Beige wall after beige wall, prickly carpeting, narrow hallways, low ceilings, few windows, and cold, concrete-covered outsides act like a lead blanket laid over the spirits of the inhabitants. Just as beauty feeds the souls of those who see it, the lack of beauty starves us of something we have difficulty describing but keenly feel. Where is the life? The worth? The loving process?

God's highest value is not efficiency, especially not in any simple or mechanistic sense—it is *love*. He is more interested in beauty than the speed of progress; he is more concerned to lift our gaze, to provoke song, and to stimulate our imaginations than he is to just get things done. God is not wasteful or negligent; rather, he's purposeful and wise, patient and intentional as he works.

Wouldn't it have been much more efficient for God to create the entire world in a single color? What if everything God made was gray or shades of black and white? Someone shaped by the modern industrial mindset might negatively assess God as indulgent, wasteful, and excessive. Why the extravagance of a peacock's feathers, the careful complexity of the orchid, the multilayered nature of the human voice, or the transcendence of an orgasm? Sure, we can offer explanations for each of these,

> The Spirit is the source of the love of God that is the root of all flourishing life.
>
> —Miroslav Volf and Matthew Croasmun, *For the Life of the World: Theology That Makes a Difference* (Grand Rapids: Brazos, 2019), 180.

but was it really necessary to have so many colors, so much diversity, so much depth, so much wonder? Why? Because God is not driven by efficiency alone.

Love, beauty, wonder, and worship are God's main goals. Sometimes he is astonishingly quick in his work. He can quickly turn water to wine. He can make a dead person rise. But often, like a creative and brilliant architect who is compelled by love rather than mere production, God takes slower routes. Exodus normally takes time, calling for faith and growth. Process has always been God's normal pattern. Rather than snapping his fingers, the Father, through his Word, sends the Spirit over the darkness, hovering above turbulent waters while beginning to bring order out of the emptiness and the void (Gen. 1:2). The God who has always valued process is thus more characterized by love than mere productivity or efficiency.

Love, community, and growth of character are often—though not always—at odds with our notions of efficiency. One of the most *in*efficient things you can ever do is love another person—or even a puppy. Loving another creature requires engagement, response, and patience. Loads of patience. Similarly, the artist or author knows all too well that efficiency is often the enemy, rather than the friend, of creativity and progress. The almighty Creator, however, has always been comfortable prioritizing love and growth over efficiency and check marks. I want to be more like him!

QUESTIONS FOR REFLECTION

- Do you find yourself valuing efficiency and productivity as your highest goods? How do you see God in Scripture provide a different narrative?

- How might considering God as the great Architect— who intended his creation to display depth, beauty, and

slow growth—influence your view of efficiency, progress, and productivity? How might this change your
expectations about personal growth in grace and truth?
Consider whether God is asking you to extend more
patience and grace to others (and yourself!) than you do
currently.

- Read John 7. Notice Jesus's remarks in verses 6 and
  8 about "my time." What difference does his timing
  make to his ministry in this chapter? What processes in-
  volving time affect the crowds who hear him?

Communion Is the Goal of Being Human

Eschatology aims at consummation rather than restoration.
—Geerhardus Vos, *The Eschatology of the Old Testament*

Humans were originally designed for communion with God, with each other, and with the rest of the created world. A quick look at Genesis 1 shows us that time, like finitude, is another good aspect of creation; it also shows us that the goodness increases from day to day. An increase in goodness through time also takes the form of growth, and it isn't hard to imagine how God would value the goodness of growth over time.

Communion itself is a process, it takes time, and it results in growth. It could also be described as an embodied love, engaging the whole of our being. We do not merely *have* bodies or faculties (i.e., minds, wills, affections); rather, as embodied psychosomatic creatures, we invest in relationships that define us by means of our bodies and faculties: we hug, we laugh, we serve, we honor. Our bodies and our faculties were designed to express love.

Unfortunately, we tend to value speed over plodding, we honor individual glory over communal unity, and we prize industrial productivity over relational fidelity. These values undermine love and communion. John Swinton, author of a wonderful volume titled *Becoming Friends of Time: Disability, Timefullness, and Gentle Discipleship*, recognizes that the presence of those with profound intellectual disabilities often causes our communities to display what we really believe but seldom admit: your worth is tied to your productivity, or your value is linked to your IQ. This judgment isn't pretty. The church has not fully resisted the temptation to adopt efficiency-driven systems of value, which distort our vision and experience of communion.

Christians often feel guilty or ashamed about their limited intellectual abilities or physical weaknesses, or how their will-power fluctuates with their blood sugar levels. For example, are you an unfaithful Christian if you fall short of Michael Jordan's fanatical drivenness and competitive willpower on the court? Or should we be reminded that mere exercises of determination were never the heart of the Christian concern about self-control? Christianity is discipleship unto Jesus, not an endless self-improvement program, strength training, or better education. Its goal has always been *to grow in love and communion with God, neighbors, and the rest of his creation.* This is true no matter one's cognitive, physical, or emotional

As this God-given rest soaks my soul, there are these tender sprouts of gratitude poking their way up through the surface of my consciousness, and I find myself feeling grateful for aspects of my life I have taken for granted all week when life was too full and yet empty all at the same time.

—Ruth Haley Barton, *Embracing Rhythms of Work and Rest: From Sabbath to Sabbatical and Back Again* (Downers Grove, IL: InterVarsity, 2022), 67.

challenges. To appreciate this, we need to consider afresh the full humanity of Christ.

Jesus did not just drop out of heaven as an adult, ready to jump onto a cross. Instead, as the mediator between God and humanity, the incarnate Son experienced the fullness of human life, including creaturely limits. As Irenaeus (ca. 130–202) once argued, by going through the normal seasons of human life, the Messiah was in some mysterious way going about the work of renewing creation itself.[1] With the incarnation of the Son, the infinite Creator experienced finite creaturely realities. The fact that the Gospels do not give us many details of Jesus's development—from infancy to childhood, from adolescence to early adulthood—should actually comfort us. We have no descriptions of his learning to talk or going through puberty, but we can assume he went through the awkwardness of these stages just like the rest of us. If he didn't, that would indeed be worth telling us. No, he was like us in all ways, yet without sin.

As the Gospels show us, Jesus's love for the Father and his neighbor was his most important trait, not his IQ or physical stamina. He demonstrated a genuine solidarity with the rest of us. From the tone of the records, we can assume that his life, from birth to death, was mostly filled with common physical, mental, and emotional challenges and growth. Luke, for example, makes this observation: "And the child [Jesus] grew and became strong, filled with wisdom. And the favor of God was upon him" (Luke 2:40; cf. 2:52). Growth, increase, and development, and still a human nature with limits.

As the one filled with the Spirit beyond measure (John 3:34), Jesus eventually was able to teach with unique power and authority during his years of ministry (Matt. 7:29; 9:6–8; 28:18; John 12:49; 14:10), and the culmination of his growth would be him offering *himself* as the full and final sacrifice for sin, once for all (Heb. 9:26; 10:12; cf. Eph. 5:2; Heb. 4:14–5:10). His humanity has redeemed ours!

None of us need to be Jesus; we just need to be connected to him by faith. Yet his genuine humanity also reminds us that the Creator never expects us to be superhuman, simply truly human. Whether speaking of how we were originally designed or what life in glory will be like, we can affirm that we are never more human than when we experience love and communion with God, which then has implications for how we relate to our neighbors and the rest of creation. Jesus embodied this faithful human response to the Father, and by the Spirit, we—no matter our physical, mental, or emotional challenges—in some mysterious way enter that response through faith, hope, and love.

QUESTIONS FOR REFLECTION

- Do you think that communion with God or neighbor is rushed in your everyday life? Why or why not? And if so, how does this hurried communion take shape for you?
- How comfortable are you thinking through the full humanity of Jesus? Have you ever considered the idea of his own growth and human development? What implications might his humanity have for yours?
- Read Philippians 4. Look at how important relational connections are to Paul—a connectivity that flows out of the church's relationship with Christ. What is the nature of communion in this passage?

The Normal Work of the Spirit

Christian virtue, including the ninefold fruit of the Spirit, is
both the gift of God and the result of the person of faith making conscious decisions to cultivate this way of life and these
habits of heart and mind.

—N. T. Wright, *After You Believe*

The Holy Spirit of God gives us new birth into the family of
God (John 3:3, 7; 1 Pet. 1:3, 23); new status as saints, who no
longer bow to sin as our master (e.g., Rom. 6:1–2; 1 Cor. 6:11);
and new fellowship with our new brothers and sisters (2 Cor.
13:14). But the same Spirit, the Spirit of creation, also slowly
transforms our loves and opens opportunities for communion
over time. New Testament scholar Ralph Martin explains that
according to the apostle Paul, the believer's growth is "gradual
and progressive, from one stage of glory to yet a higher stage
. . . , climaxing in the goal reached" in our glorification with
Christ (Rom. 8:17, 29–30). Paul encourages his listeners with
his expectation of seeing Christ formed in them (Gal. 4:19; cf.
Phil. 3:21; 1 John 3:2).

Now let's be clear: this growth does not occur with an un-wavering increase in godly motives, behavior, and purposes. We don't just go up, up, up. Many of us know what it feels like to sink down, down, down. Like the child learning to ride a bike, we inevitably fall, sometimes painfully crashing toward the ground and getting hurt in the process. Nor are we always the best judges of our own growth. Sometimes others see what we cannot.

Growth is often imperceptible to us, either because it is slow, or because it isn't the kind of growth that we can see, or because we don't understand it as growth, or for other reasons. A strange paradox in this growth can be found in many saints. Many of the godliest Christians have been pro-foundly aware of their sin—they have grown more, rather than less, aware of its distorting presence as the years have passed. Yet those who know them sometimes find it hard to believe that they really struggle with sin like the rest of us. Why? Because when we try to judge growth, we often apply categories of moralism rather than the biblical categories of the Spirit's fruit: love, joy, peace, patience, kindness, goodness, faithfulness, gentleness, and self-control. We live in a world that works for outward and obvious triumph, so it doesn't value slow-growing character traits like gentleness and joy. But in God's kingdom, these traits are the focal points of real growth and development.

God's Spirit continually moves and stirs us to faithfulness in communion with God, with one another, and with the world

> God is not just saving individuals and preparing them for heaven; rather, he is creating a people among whom he can live and who in their life together will reproduce God's life and character.
>
> —Gordon D. Fee, *Paul, the Spirit, and the People of God* (Peabody, MA: Hendrickson, 1996), 66.

around us. So how do we know that God's Spirit is working in us? Should we primarily look for signs or extraordinary powers? No, we should primarily look for love (see, e.g., Rom. 5:5; Gal. 5:6; 1 John 4:11–21). John Owen (1616–83) worried that extreme expectations often produce attitudes that belittle the way God has made us—as creatures with finite minds, limited emotional capacities, and the need for conscious participation in the Spirit's work within them. The question Owen wanted to ask those in his day who were emphasizing ecstatic experiences but downplaying Scripture and reason was this: Were they seeking a spirit that undermined our humanity or one that reaffirmed and strengthened it? Since the Spirit of creation is the same as the Spirit of re-creation, the work of sanctification and transformation should make us more—not less—human. A true sign of the Holy Spirit's work is the exaltation of Christ, not teeth turning gold or someone making unexpected barking noises (real examples from the history of the church!).

Since the Spirit of sanctification is the same as the Spirit of creation, we should expect that God's Spirit will not typically give us extraordinary powers but rather will redirect us toward our original end—namely, fuller communion with God. For this purpose, the Spirit gives us new hearts, provokes in us a love for God and neighbor, and strengthens us in the good deeds of love and grace. Again, marks of spiritual growth do not include how many miracles one can do or how many astonishing experiences one has had. Rather, what really matters is whether one is growing in love for God and neighbor. That is the test—the fruit!

The work of God's Spirit follows the pattern shown at creation: though sometimes his work is immediate and dramatic, more often it is slow and progressive, calling for and encouraging our agency rather than undermining it. May God's Spirit continue to grow his fruit in us.

QUESTIONS FOR REFLECTION

- Why do you think it is so common to pit the "extraordinary" work of the Spirit against the Spirit's normal patterns of work, found in sustaining, renewing, and growing his good creation?

- Have you ever considered the pace of the Spirit's work? Can you think of biblical examples where the Spirit works quickly? How about examples where the Spirit works over an extended period? What might it look like for us to value both patterns?

- First-century believers in Corinth exhibited a great variety of spiritual gifts, and yet they were often led to factions, disruption of fellowship, and contempt for one another. How might this observation inform your understanding of gifts, both in others and in yourself? For Paul's description of how the gifts should be used, reread 1 Corinthians 12. And for his admonition that love be more important than the gifts themselves, revisit 1 Corinthians 13.

So Many Needs

The "isolated individual" is the product of man's fallen imagination. It is a product of sin. It does not exist. It has no reality at all. What does exist are persons in community.

—Thomas Hopko, *All the Fulness of God*

Are the needs in God's church and world ever fully met? What should you personally do about them?

Because Christ lives in his people, we begin to feel God's compassion for the brokenness of the world. But since we don't properly take account of our creaturely limits, the extent of the needs around us can be crushing. "Compassion fatigue" describes the reaction commonly experienced when our limited capacity faces unlimited needs. What are we to do? The two options most often presented to Christians are either (1) "Do everything" or (2) "You don't need to do anything." In the next few days, we will navigate these questions, seeking a path that neither downplays the validity of the needs nor romanticizes the contributions of single individuals. We will see just how much we really do need one another—and that such need is a good thing.

Some Christians say that our only obligation to the world is to proclaim the gospel, arguing that we should narrow our focus and "only do what the Bible requires" or "simplify and be like the early church." These simple proposals are understandable, but they often rest on invalid assumptions.

Yes, simplifying might happily mean ending some unneeded or distracting programs, but in practice, it too often means ignoring concerns that are time-consuming but nonetheless very near the heart of God (e.g., caring for the poor, widows, orphans, and the lost). How, then, do we avoid ignoring the needs highlighted in Scripture due to our own blind spots? None of us approach the Bible without presuppositions and biases; instead, we tend to highlight what we are comfortable with while ignoring areas that make us uncomfortable. Those of us, for example, who haven't personally faced material poverty, regular patterns of injustice, or ongoing physical suffering can have a hard time seeing how often the Bible addresses these problems. Clearly, we should not confuse our lack of attention with God's lack of concern. Furthermore, because needs can be so vast and complex, affluent and busy parishioners like me, for example, are tempted to harden our hearts to the poor. But this doesn't mean that God himself has hardened his heart to the poor or that his church should.

In the first century, Christians did not just preach and pray (although those were central); they also shared their goods, cared for widows, comforted the grieving, strengthened the poor, testified to the good news with their neighbors, and modeled a way of living in the world that contrasted with the

---

Compassion is born when we discover in the center of our existence not only that God is God and man is man, but also that our neighbor is really our fellow man.

—Henri J. M. Nouwen, *The Wounded Healer* (New York: Doubleday, 1972), 41.

culture around them (cf. Acts 2:42–47). With bread and wine, the church uniquely offered a heavenly taste of shalom that broke into a hungry and hurting world. It displayed hope by bringing the light and peace of Christ to bear on real pain and need. The church candidly addressed sin and dysfunction, leading to repentance and healing. People experienced shalom as the Spirit of God brought fresh waves of grace, unity, and love to and through God's people.

We shouldn't be surprised, therefore, that those who are filled with the Spirit want to help a hurting world in all kinds of creative ways, with words and actions. The spiritually poor *and* materially poor *and* relationally poor are all legitimate objects of care for those who worship the Creator and Redeemer.

The good news of Christ produces a holistic view of the world in us, driving our affections and actions with compassion. Our culture may tempt us to forget the elderly, who are no longer productive, but the church must remember and include them. The world may tempt us to ignore vulnerable babies in the womb, but the church must tend to them too. Our subcultures tempt us to befriend people who share our economic or educational background, but the church requires more from us. Oppression and division between people of different ethnic backgrounds or contrasting skin colors may sound too "political" and secular for our gatherings, but the church must resist such dismissals and instead love across all boundaries.

Today, we have been reminded that legitimate needs are worth acknowledging and addressing. Yes, God calls us to care beyond our ability to do so. In tomorrow's reflection, we will see that in order to fulfill this call, our methods of care must be much more about "we" than "me." In other words, a more communal response from God's people not only faithfully reflects Scripture's emphasis, it also provides a pathway that is sustainable and life-giving for all involved.

QUESTIONS FOR REFLECTION

- Imagine you are sitting down with Jesus, and you ask him, "What needs in this world should Christians care about?" What do you think he would say? And why?

- How can you begin to have your heart broken over the things that break God's heart?

- In your experience, do you think the church has under-emphasized, overemphasized, or offered a good balance with respect to major social concerns, such as suffering, poverty, and injustice? What have you seen that is positive, and in what ways might the church be more holistic and faithful? Do you tend to feel overwhelmed or dismissive of the needs around you and throughout the world?

- In Mark 6, Jesus teaches, heals some people, and feeds others. But he works in these specific ways and not others. Why? How might this help you embrace your own limits and find contentment in the specific work that God has for you?

Should the Church Care about More Than Souls?

Authentic community-in-Christ, in its global and local visible presence in the world, is a political community embodying, demonstrating, and proclaiming the politics of the good news of the reign of God.

—D. Zac Niringiye,
"Churches and the Politics of the Sacraments"

Because we worship King Jesus, who has brought us into his kingdom, the gospel is inherently political and social, although mostly not in ways that our surrounding culture would understand. We are part of a kingdom in which people from all tribes, tongues, skin colors, and cultures come together to worship the living God. Prejudices and blind spots about race, class, and ability too often hinder our unity and are occasions for repentance and restitution—as when Zacchaeus returned to his neighbors the money he gained from an oppressive system (Luke 19:1–10).

As Proverbs states, "Speak up and judge fairly; defend the rights of the poor and needy" (31:9 NIV). In other words, those who have experienced the love of the Father, the grace of the Son, and the fellowship of the Holy Spirit are called to a broad range of concerns and actions. Such a call has corporate and individual sides, but it is undeniably a call to do the good work God has prepared for us (Eph. 2:10), including letting him who is "our peace" overcome our hostilities and bring together "strangers and aliens" as one in him (2:13–22). This is not merely about affirming theological statements but about reforming how we order our lives, friendships, and pocketbooks.

To be concerned that God's will be carried out on earth as it is in heaven is a gospel issue, central to the Christian mission and to the church. When we ignore the difficulty that some people have in obtaining their daily bread, or we think that accumulated debt has no spiritual import, or we believe we can hold grudges against individuals or groups without consequence, then we distance ourselves from God and from many for whom he deeply cares (cf. Matt. 6:9–15).

At the core of the church's being and nature is love for God and neighbor. Our allegiance as the church is always to the King and his kingdom, not to any earthly political party. To the

---

Community is like a large mosaic. Each little piece seems so insignificant. One piece is bright red, another cold blue or dull green, another warm purple, another sharp yellow, another shining gold. Some look precious, others ordinary. Some look valuable, others worthless. . . . As individual stones, we can do little with them except compare them and judge their beauty and value. When, however, all these little stones are brought together in one big mosaic portraying the face of Christ, who would ever question the importance of any one of them? If one of them, even the least spectacular one, is missing, the face is incomplete. Together in the one mosaic, each little stone is indispensable and makes a unique contribution to the glory of God.

—Henri J. M. Nouwen, *Can You Drink the Cup?* (Notre Dame, IN: Ave Maria, 1996), 58.

extent that our life together as the church reflects this allegiance, we can show the rest of the world the goodness of our Lord and give them an appetite for the fellowship that we will one day fully enjoy with him. In other words, the good news that Jesus is Lord has ramifications for all areas of life, but faithfulness in hearing and responding to that good news takes the whole church, not just an individual.

Yes, there are all kinds of good and important works to be done. Preaching (Matt. 24:14; Rom. 10:14; 1 Tim. 4:13; 2 Tim. 3:16; 4:2), prayer (2 Chron. 7:14; Matt. 18:19–20; Acts 2:42; 2 Cor. 1:11; James 5:16), and participating in the sacraments (Matt. 26:26–28; 28:19; 1 Cor. 10:16–17; 11:23–25) are like the body's skeleton, supporting and uniting all efforts that flow from God through his church to the world. That skeleton, however, is *not* all that the church and Christians are called to; the body is much more than its bones. From sermon preparation to evangelism, from shared meals to preparing the elements for the Eucharist, from concern for children to the dignity of elder care, from caring for orphans to speaking on behalf of the voiceless, there is so much work (most of it behind the scenes) that helps a healthy believing community gather and flourish together (cf. Rom. 12:11–13; Heb. 10:24–25).

We need our imaginations renewed to better envision the grand and full implications of the gospel for this hurting and broken world. When Jesus came, his messianic significance was captured with the following description sent to the imprisoned John the Baptist: "Go and tell John what you have seen and heard: the blind receive their sight, the lame walk, lepers are cleansed, and the deaf hear, the dead are raised up, the poor have good news preached to them" (Luke 7:22; cf. Matt. 11:5). This portrayal doesn't merely indicate that Jesus could do amazing things, as if miracles alone were proof that he was the Messiah. No, it tells us that the Creator is caring for his creation, that the eternal Son's mission brings all manner of healing to this rebellious and hurting world. Both in this messianic description of Jesus and in the early church's response to the resurrected Christ (Acts 2:42–47), we see that the gospel addresses both body and soul. The Creator is both our Redeemer and our Sustainer: the triune God not only deals with sins but also cares for our physical pains, relational isolation, and spiritual hardness. God's ultimate goal is not merely forgiveness but also healing and full human flourishing.

QUESTIONS FOR REFLECTION

- Do you find it difficult to reconcile caring for people's souls on the one hand, and providing for physical needs on the other? If so, describe that tension or feeling. Can you see how discounting physical needs may cause you to feel distanced from God?

- Might God be calling your local church to increased proclamation or increased demonstrations of material concern for others? Can you imagine creative ways in which your leadership might encourage and empower congregants to such efforts without employing shame and guilt, so that the church might serve and minister with joy? What would that look like?

- Returning to Mark 6 (from yesterday's reflections), how did Jesus minister to both body and soul?

What Is the Church's Mission?

Man appears to exist in his ecclesial identity not as that which
he is but as that which he will be.

—John Zizioulas, *Being as Communion*

The central mission of the church is to point people continually
to the Messiah; he alone fully reveals the love of the Father and
pours out his Spirit on us. The goal of all our good efforts is to
draw people to the embrace of the triune God, not to serve as a
replacement for him. All the gifts we exercise must ultimately
point back to the true Giver. So how can all of this happen?

The church is central to Christian existence. As hard as it can
be to believe sometimes, the church is also God's normal means
of expressing his presence, love, and grace in his world. God
extends his love, provision, and values through the people who
make up the body of Christ. Thus, God's offer to be a refuge
and strength frequently comes through the church. When he
wants to bring a word of grace, a safe hug, and a warm meal,
it often comes through his church. Although the church cannot
do everything itself, it keeps promoting the common good in
whatever ways it can. But it does make mistakes.

Sometimes individual Christians have imagined that they must personally reflect the fullness of Jesus the Messiah. Whether third-century hermits or contemporary pastors and activists, they've imagined—often without realizing it—that they must personally fulfill messianic expectations. This illusion has become even more intense in the modern Western world, with its stress on individual faith and personal responsibility. If those instincts are unconnected to a robust view of the communal nature of the church, they can lead to destructive results.

We see such results in the story of Charles Thomas Studd (1860–1931), who served as an English evangelical missionary. He wanted to give his whole life to Christ and spread the gospel, serving in China, India, and eventually Africa. Giving up financial and educational privilege, he poured himself out in his work. His belief that Christ gave up everything for him spurred him to practice what he called "reckless Christianity," which brought not only heroic stories but also some destructive consequences. His untiring devotion to the work became somewhat fanatical (at least as others experienced it). For example, by the end of his life, he was working eighteen hours a day and was addicted to morphine. During the last thirteen years of his marriage, he only saw his wife for two weeks despite her struggling health, and he even dismissed his daughter and son-in-law from the mission because they did not show the same level of commitment that he did. He admitted that this period of intense struggle was his "Gethsemane," which seems revealing, for it showed that he sensed that he was required to

A church that lives in line with God's justice *proclaims the kingdom of God by its very life.*

—Michael J. Rhodes, *Just Discipleship: Biblical Justice in an Unjust World*
(Downers Grove, IL: IVP Academic, 2023), 282.

> If there was no other way of their relief, those that have the lightest
> burden might be obliged still to take some of his neighbor's burden,
> to make his burden more supportable. A brother may be obliged to
> help a brother in extremity, though they are both very much in want.
>
> —Jonathan Edwards, *The Works of Jonathan Edwards*, vol. 17, *Sermons and Discourses,*
> *1730–1733*, ed. Mark Valeri (New Haven: Yale University Press, 1999), 398.

follow the exact path of Christ and to do all that was required
of Jesus. At one point, he admitted, "My heart seems worn out
and bruised beyond repair, and in my deep loneliness I often
wish to be gone."[1]

Is such reckless Christianity required of us? If we don't follow such a radical life, whether in missions, social justice, or
proclamation, is it because we don't take the demands of God
seriously enough? What may have sounded godly and impressive
at first can quickly devolve into arrogant and isolating behavior
that substitutes zeal and conquest for love and relational
wholeness.

Such well-meaning inclinations often demonstrate (1) how
we underestimate the uniqueness of Christ and his work,
(2) how we overestimate God's expectations for each individual
(finite!) human being, and (3) how we underestimate the work
of Christ in his body, the church. While it is vital to remember
that Jesus died for us (redemption), we must also remember that
God originally made us good, even with our limits (creation),
and that he draws us to mutual dependence on one another for
spiritual health (ecclesiology—the church!). We don't take these
truths into account nearly as much as we should.

So where does this leave us? Are we back to the binary—do
everything in an effort to be like Jesus, or do *nothing* because
Jesus's blood has covered our sins and shortcomings? How are
we to take seriously the story of the sheep and the goats (Matt.
25:31–46) without either dismissing it or being crushed by it?

Earlier we stated that the doctrine of creation indicates another path for us. Combining a robust doctrine of creation with a fuller focus on Christ and the church will make this possibility clearer. We turn to that tomorrow.

QUESTIONS FOR REFLECTION

- Jesus is the Good Shepherd, who laid down his life for his sheep (John 10:11–18), and we receive forgiveness and life in him. Yet in Matthew 25:31–46, Jesus tells the judgment story of the sheep and the goats, who are distinguished by what they've done to "the least of these" (e.g., the hungry, naked, sick, imprisoned, and marginalized, vv. 40, 45). The sheep have served these people, reflecting the heart of the Shepherd, while the goats have not. How might we understand this narrative without making it seem like we earn our own salvation?

- Have you ever seen the church faithfully represent Christ's care, comfort, and grace? How has this encouraged or shaped you?

- We are called to follow Christ and imitate him, yet our salvation and hope rests not on our faithfulness but on his. How might the church honor this dynamic without undermining the radical nature of grace or downplaying the good work God has prepared for his people? Can you think of churches that have done this well? What did it look like?

It Takes the Entire Community
to Reflect the One Messiah

Human beings exist in duality, and it is in this dependence on
the other that their creatureliness consists.

—Dietrich Bonhoeffer, *Creation and Fall*

The *whole* church is called the body of Christ (e.g., 1 Cor.
12:12–27), not as a collection of isolated people but as a united
organism: "We, though many, are one body in Christ, and indi-
vidually members one of another" (Rom. 12:5). The *one* body
of Christ consists of the *whole* church, and that body is com-
posed of great diversity and difference, each member dependent
not only on Christ but also on one another.

This understanding of the church is easily lost in our individualistic culture. Consequently, believers with individualistic
expectations are overloaded when they try to fulfill all the biblical injunctions alone. Jesus wasn't joking when he said the
thing that separated the sheep and the goats was what they
did for "the least of these," including feeding the hungry, caring for the stranger, clothing the naked, helping the sick, and

visiting prisoners (Matt. 25:31–46). When the church responds as a *community*—as a united body—to the Spirit's life-giving power, we are liberated to act faithfully and effectively. Or to use Irwyn Ince's apt description, we become the "beautiful community," reflecting our beautiful God.[1] None of us alone can do all that God commands his people, but none of us were ever meant to do that alone anyway.

You and I are not the Messiah. Nor is your pastor the Messiah. But *together*, abiding in the finished work of Christ and empowered by the Spirit, we can carry out the Father's compassion and love by participating in his holy work. We do this as the body of Christ.

For example, I can't pray for everyone who needs prayer, but as part of this body, Christians throughout the world can pray together for all who need prayer. Furthermore, this work also requires the contributions of those who have secular vocations, who honor Christ as painters and teachers, as landscapers and homemakers, as politicians and software engineers. We all need one another.

Scottish theologian John Baillie (1886–1960) captures this spirit when he prays, "O Lord of the vineyard, I beg Thy blessing upon all who truly desire to serve Thee by being diligent and faithful in their several callings, *bearing their due share of the world's burden*, and going about their daily tasks in all simplicity and uprightness of heart."[2] He goes on to pray for

---

The church is birthed by the kingdom of God and is meant both to bear witness to the kingdom and to reflect its values. As believers serve one another, representing Christ to one another, broken but redeemed persons engage other broken persons with the redemptive love of Christ to bring personal and communal transformation.

—Brad Harper and Paul Louis Metzger, *Exploring Ecclesiology: An Evangelical and Ecumenical Introduction* (Grand Rapids: Brazos, 2009), 158–59.

those in various vocations, from farmers to shepherds, from those entering dark mines to those employed in factories and the marketplace. Whether we buy or sell, use pens or the plow, tend the hearth or the child, we all can use our labor to honor God and seek the common good.

Accepting our finitude and affirming our interdependence as the people of God moves us from guilt to liberty, from passivity to activity, from being overwhelmed to being energized. God does not call each of us to do everything—after all, he is the one who gave us our limits! He also uniquely gifted and called each of us to some form of service and love. This calling is not reserved simply for the "spiritual" people in full-time church ministry—this is an invitation and a calling for all of us.

We are not rugged individuals; we are an interconnected body. Jesus does not overburden his flock; he affirms who they are in their life as a whole. "You are in me, and I am in you," he says (John 14:20 NIV), which is also true of our participation in one another as a body. A part is not the whole; nor should the whole be reduced to the part. This is why we weep with those who weep, why we celebrate with those who celebrate. We serve and we feast, we rest and we labor, we love and we sacrifice. Living in Christ means that we imitate him, but *it takes the whole church to fully reflect the Messiah.*

Only Jesus is his whole body. Only he is the Messiah. The rest of us don't have to be him; we just have to be *in* him, united to one another as his body.

QUESTIONS FOR REFLECTION

- How has God gifted you? Have you considered what your "due share" of burdens might be in this season of life? What expectations do you think Jesus has for you?

Do you sense that certain forms of radical individualism have misshaped your expectations or experiences?

- How connected do you feel to your church community? How might you help foster healthy interconnectedness there? How well does your community celebrate different gifts and responsibilities?
- How might this emphasis on mutual dependence and interconnectedness aid our witness to the watching world? How might it influence our presentations of the gospel?

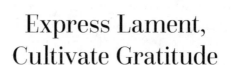

Express Lament,
Cultivate Gratitude

As for me, I call to God, and the LORD saves me. Evening,
morning and noon I cry out in distress, and he hears my voice.

—Psalm 55:16–17 (NIV)

One of the remarkable things that Scripture affirms is that two
conflicting truths in life can exist at the same time: problems and
frustrations coexist with gifts from God. Acknowledging both our
frustrations and our delights often requires courage and patience.
How do we do so as Christians? Through lament and gratitude.

Both our secular culture and the church often push us to
choose between things that are equally true. Dichotomies and
tensions are constantly before us, asking us to pick a winner:
the individual or the community, grace or effort, piety or cultural engagement, love or justice, lament or gratitude. What if,
instead of choosing an unrealistic oversimplification, we choose
biblical realism? This posture would allow us to express both
sorrow and thanksgiving, each a genuine part of our experience
and neither canceling out the other.

We develop biblical gratitude and joy not by ignoring the bad but by ensuring that our vision is not reduced to a single mood. Looking for signs of God's presence and provision, we grow attentive to beauty and life even amid the real challenges and hurts. Embracing this dynamic helps us resist two pressures. Some people tell us that believers are always supposed to be happy and filled with gratitude, but their approach to pain and suffering is simply to deny or downplay it. This refusal of the real is neither honest nor helpful. Others, however, are so aware of the hurts and problems in this life that expressions of joy or gratitude appear to them naive at best or coldhearted at worst. Yet in light of God's compassion, his provision in Christ, and the beauty of his creation, we have genuine reasons to be grateful.

So what does life look like if we don't have to pick between lament and joy?

It is appropriate that we express honest lament in the face of hardship, injustice, and suffering. Lament does not deny faith in God but actually expresses faith—you don't voice frustration, confusion, or pain to someone who isn't there. As the psalmist says, "My God, my God, why . . . ?" (Ps. 22:1). This verse addresses not a distant deity but David's God, the Lord of the covenant, Israel's sovereign King, who is present and listening—as the rest of the psalm testifies. This is the Almighty, who has made promises, who is good and trustworthy. This is *my* God. *I*, as an individual, and *we*, as a people, cry out to this God and no other. So when we hurt, when we have deep questions, when we see atrocities and experience slights, we

For Paul, thanksgiving has a performative effect on the things received. Receiving God's gifts with thanks does not merely identify them as gifts but also sanctifies them, consecrates them as holy things. The world is sanctified, made holy, through thanks.

—Peter J. Leithart, *Gratitude: An Intellectual History* (Waco: Baylor University Press, 2014), 72.

Because there is no room in the church for our negative experiences [through lament], not only are we ill-prepared when tragedy strikes, but people also learn to deny their true feelings. Since there is no room for their negative experiences, they learn to hide these. They feel obligated to create their own "virtual identity"—the "always OK" image.

—Federico G. Villanueva, *It's OK to Be Not OK: Preaching the Lament Psalms*
(Carlisle, UK: Langham Preaching Resources, 2017), 7.

lament, believing that his presence, compassion, and power can handle our raw emotions without being overwhelmed by them.

Lament and thanksgiving are not in a contest. The Bible calls us to both, so don't pick between Psalms 22 and 23. Believers are allowed to cry in their distress, "My God, my God, why have you forsaken me?" (22:1), and at the same time, they can confidently declare, "The LORD is my shepherd" (23:1). These expressions are not tied to good and bad times but to the one God, who is present in both; we gain confidence in God's kindness and provision when we "walk through the valley of the shadow of death" (v. 4). If we choose one expression and not both, we risk turning our laments into hopeless despair or reducing divine promises to shallow clichés. When we express both lament and gratitude, each becomes stronger and truer.

Now to the key point: *lament and gratitude are mirror concepts that highlight the same fundamental truth: we depend on the God who rescues us.* Only when we accept our creaturely finitude will this make sense to us. When life is hard, troubling, and wrong, we lean on God, voicing our fears and frustrations to the Creator and Sustainer. We depend on him to make right what is wrong, to heal what is diseased, to repair what is broken, to forgive what sins have been committed. Likewise, when a newborn is put into the arms of her mother, when a scrumptious meal feeds the body, when laughter strengthens the soul, when injustice is corrected, and when our work is done well—in all of this, we rejoice and express gratitude, for it reminds us that God is the giver of all good gifts and that we depend on him for life, breath, and our very existence.

We live in this tension. We might be thankful for a loved one's peaceful passing, even as we experience deep sorrow and loss. We may be overjoyed that our child got into college, while simultaneously feeling a knot in our stomachs as we cannot imagine how we will pay for it. We can be happy for a friend's promotion and, in the same moment, feel the pain of being overlooked ourselves. God created in us an intricate web of emotional responses. *Lament and gratitude together not only recognize our dependence on God, they also deepen our sense of his faithfulness.*

QUESTIONS FOR REFLECTION

- We are all born with different temperaments, so we often respond to life differently. Accordingly, does gratitude or lament come more naturally to you? Why do you think the less natural response is more difficult to experience and express?
- How might Christian expressions of gratitude and lament differ from the kinds of things advocated in contemporary self-help books?
- Try to recall a passage in the Gospels when Jesus expresses gratitude, as well as a passage when he expresses lament. What might it mean that both lament and gratitude were realities in our Savior's very human life? How might we imitate and take comfort from Jesus's joy and lament?
- Read Psalms 22 and 23 again. How does each psalm express both lament and gratitude?
- Use the psalms to help guide you in a lament (e.g., Pss. 6, 13, 44, 69, 130). What would it look like to implement laments in your life—writing them, reading them, or even singing them?

Embracing the Rhythms
and Seasons of Life

> Time is God's gift. Only time given and received as a gift is
> real time.
>
> —Eberhard Busch, *The Great Passion*

Kate Bowler, in her moving memoir *Everything Happens for
a Reason, and Other Lies I've Loved*, walks readers through
her heartbreaking struggle with cancer (among other things).
She describes her love of anticipating "the next thing," always
planning, always improving, always making things better. She
was constantly planning for the future, longing for what was
to come. While anticipation is often beneficial for us, she came
to see that it has a dark side at times, a side she calls "the sin of
arrogance, of becoming impervious to life itself." She adds, "I
failed to love what was present, and decided to love what was
possible instead. I must learn to live in ordinary time, but I don't
know how." Our circumstances are inevitably different, but I
believe that Bowler senses here some fairly common challenges:
appreciating the present, honoring our limits as we invest and

grow, and loving what God has given rather than feeling angry about what is withheld or anxious about what is to come.

Might one of our greatest challenges be that when we judge how we are doing, we try to assess the whole by only looking at a part? What I mean is this: we imagine what a faithful and rich life looks like (often visualizing a romanticized future we never seem to arrive at); then, on any given morning, we compare that idealized vision with the incomplete person we see staring back at us in the mirror, and we end up disliking the person we are in that moment. We see bags under our eyes and anticipate a day of laying bricks or cleaning or being stuck in endless and un-fruitful meetings. We don't feel strong or triumphant; we don't feel significant or accomplished; we just feel small and tired.

Trying to "have it all" pushes us to expect that we should, every day, experience the whole of life and not just a part. So we take the hopes and ambitions of a lifetime, of a year, of a month, of a week, and we shove them into each and every day. That, as I know all too well, is a recipe for disaster. Rather than cultivating a life of gratitude and joy, it produces frustration and resentment. What if we (re)learned how to live by the seasonal nature of life? What if we learned to appreciate the rhythms of the day, of the weeks, of the years?

How are we to know if we are faithful? Well, we probably need to be more realistic about what to expect of ourselves

In the Christian practice of living through the year, recurring patterns of longing and fulfillment, or repentance and grace, encircle us again and again as we encounter different dimensions of the mystery of God at each point in time, all year long. Over time, the round years accumulate into a thick line, and we find that we have been caught up in the story of God.

—Dorothy C. Bass, *Receiving the Day: Christian Practices for Opening the Gift of Time* (San Francisco: Wiley & Sons, 2000), 82.

in any given day, week, month, and year; but we also need to look beyond the immediate to a greater horizon. When we step back to imagine things from God's perspective, we might get a fresh view of what a faithful and rich life looks like; my guess is that it is much slower, more ordinary and earthy, but also more beautiful than we anticipate.

I first heard the phrase "productivity shame" from Jocelyn K. Glei, as she explored how many of us perpetually set unrealistic goals and then feel guilty about not meeting them. This has resonated deeply with me. As Glei reflects, "Creative labor has its own pace, and all you can do for the most part is show up and be present and ready to execute, if and when the insights come. But how you feel about that work and how you feel about that pace is completely within your control—it is about mindset and expectations."[1] From a Christian perspective, when our expectations ignore our limits, we are sinning, for we are trying to act as a god rather than as a human, infinite rather than finite. Harmonizing our expectations with the seasons and rhythms of life is fundamental to faithfulness. It allows us to both anticipate the future with hope and cultivate an appreciation for the present, which includes honoring process, slowness, and growth.

QUESTIONS FOR REFLECTION

- Consider this: If a friend shared how frustrated they've been with how little they've gotten done recently (even as they've tried to "use their time well"), do you think you would express compassion and gently encourage them? If so, do you find yourself extending that same level of grace to yourself? If not, why not?
- Jesus was always in perfect communion with his Father by the Spirit. And yet Jesus went through all the seasons

and stages of life, day by day. We enter this everyday communion with God by the Spirit and through the Son. How might this communion, then, be more "ordinary" than we tend to think?

- A person's main vocation (which may or may not comprise paid work) takes up most of their time. This vocation could be as a teacher, lawyer, stay-at-home parent, or construction tradesperson. What role do you think labor plays in the Christian life, and how do our limits influence our unconscious beliefs about the value of work?

- How can understanding and embracing your limits within your work help harmonize your expectations in your current season of life?

- Read Luke 2:39–52, a passage that comments on Jesus's infancy and childhood. What was this season of Christ's life like? What purposes for it are mentioned in the text?

Recognizing Our Vulnerability

To be human *is* to be vulnerable.

—Curt Thompson,
The Soul of Shame

Brené Brown gave a TED Talk called "The Power of Vulnerability" in 2010. It has been watched over sixty-six million times (!) as of September 2024. Brown's research concerning shame has produced many helpful books and promoted much-needed discussions. Her basic thesis is that pretending to be invulnerable fails us, producing lives suffocated by fear and shame, and that only by being more honest, open, and realistic about our struggles and limits can we experience any sense of wholeness.[1]

Christian psychiatrist Curt Thompson has also argued that the remedy for shame is to admit our vulnerability—that is, to recognize that we are not self-sufficient, that we are subject to coming up short, that we need others, and that we're susceptible to attack and even failure. Only by recognizing this state of vulnerability can we be fully known. We tend to think of vulnerability, however, as an occasional feeling, as when we lose our job or someone breaks up with us. Yet as Thompson rightly explains, "Vulnerability is not something we choose or that is true in a given moment, while the rest of the time it is not. Rather, it is something we *are*. This is why we wear clothes, live in houses and have speed limits. So much of what we do in life is designed, among other things, to protect us from the fact that we are vulnerable *at all times*."[2]

Just like humility, vulnerability is a real aspect of our creaturely limits and interdependence. To recognize our vulnerability is to confess that we are creatures rather than the Creator. But we fear that admitting vulnerability will either make us targets or cripple us with anxiety, so instead of seeing it as something to accept and even celebrate, we try to deny or overcome it.

Although these ideas resonate with some people, others find them very discomforting. For example, when you hear the word "vulnerable," does it sound more feminine than masculine to you? Why is this word associated more often with women than with men, at least in Western culture? It shouldn't be. To be vulnerable, to have weaknesses and needs, is not just a trendy idea; it is a part of how God has made all of us, irrelevant of gender.

By "vulnerable," I don't mean that humans are fragile. One can sympathize with the "antifragility" movements that call for greater resilience in youth and yet, at the same time, affirm our genuine vulnerability. Parents who overprotect their children imagine they can somehow shield them from all difficulties and hardships; but they and their children are inherently vulnerable creatures, not fragile but limited, flawed, and even subject to failure and susceptible to attack. Ironically, the admission of

To be loved but not known is comforting but superficial. To be known and not loved is our greatest fear. But to be fully known and truly loved is, well, a lot like being loved by God. It is what we need more than anything. It liberates us from pretense, humbles us out of our self-righteousness, and fortifies us for any difficulty life can throw at us.

—Timothy Keller, *The Meaning of Marriage: Facing the Complexities of Commitment with the Wisdom of God* (New York: Penguin, 2013), 95.

our vulnerability can help us strengthen ourselves and our children, and it can lead us to depend on each other and on God. Bumps and bruises, disappointments and challenges—they all teach us what our limits are and how to respond to them. At its best, admitting our vulnerability enables a healthy, honest, and accurate assessment of our existence, which includes authentic dependence on God, neighbor, and the earth.

God has made us dependent on his good work and on the abilities of other people, so affirming and encouraging those gifts is simply a realistic approach to life. Before God, we are always the ones in need. He alone is our safe shelter and security. He has no needs, so we can be fully honest before him, knowing he will always faithfully care for us and never manipulate or abuse us.

QUESTIONS FOR REFLECTION

- In what ways might modern, idealized views of independence distort our understanding of how vulnerable our bodies, relationships, and lives actually are? How might this observation help us better appreciate normal creaturely life?

- How does God view your vulnerability? While we don't need to express our vulnerabilities to everyone, God fully knows our situation and the depth and breadth of our needs. Therefore, how might a growing appreciation of genuine vulnerability foster spiritual growth?

- Can you remember a time when vulnerability gave you an opportunity to show humility and deepen relationships? Similarly, can you remember a time when you tried to deny or mask how vulnerable you were? In what kinds of situations has such masking been helpful, and when has it been hurtful?

- Read Matthew 4:1–11. In what ways does Jesus acknowledge his vulnerability? How does that acknowledgment help him?

Rejoice, God Is Near

Rejoice in the Lord always; again I will say, Rejoice. Let your gentleness be known to everyone. The Lord is near. Do not worry about anything, but in everything by prayer and supplication with thanksgiving let your requests be made known to God. And the peace of God, which surpasses all understanding, will guard your hearts and your minds in Christ Jesus.

—Philippians 4:4–7 (NRSV)

The Bible uses a cluster of words related to the idea of thankfulness: "rejoice," "praise," "joy," "thanksgiving," "gratitude," and others. While each word has its own nuances, they are all in the same theological and existential family. They all point to our recognition that God is the great Giver, for "*from* him and *through* him and *to* him are all things" (Rom. 11:36). Recognizing and confessing his faithfulness provokes praise, admiration, thanksgiving, and a disposition of gratitude. All of these ideas illuminate dynamics of living within a healthy sense of appreciation for God, others, and the rest of creation.

In Philippians 4:4–7, Paul begins with the imperative "Rejoice." This is less of a request and more of a directive. We are to be the kind of people who rejoice, who praise God in all seasons. Notice that Paul does not restrict rejoicing to enjoyable circumstances. But how could he rejoice without ignoring or lying about the genuine hardships of life?

Paul's answer is as simple as it is transformative: "The Lord is near" (Phil. 4:5 NRSV). Commentators debate what "near" means here, whether it describes the Lord's expected coming, which could be very soon (near in *time*), or his current proximity to us (near in *space*). But why choose? As Gordon Fee states, Paul is probably using an "intentional double entendre"; in other words, the Lord's being "at hand" includes both of these ideas.[1] I would add that Paul here exemplifies the believer who lives in the "fear of the Lord." Remember, such fear is not so much about living in fear of divine punishment as it is about living in awe of divine presence. This awe is what separates the foolish from the wise: one ignores God while the other lives in constant awareness of his nearness. Not surprisingly, then, Paul adds that our "gentleness"—or our "reasonableness" (ESV)— should be "known to everyone" (v. 5 NRSV). Those who really believe God to be near are not panicked people, not cruel or easily angered, but reasonable and even gentle.

In verse 6 of this passage, Paul encourages us not to be anxious. Why? Not because we will escape difficulty, nor because we can predict how everything will work out. After all, we are still finite! No, we can only cease to be anxious because the infinite God is with us in every situation. We are not alone. We are

We must look at ourselves as God has looked upon us and look at others in the same way. God made us with faces so his could shine on ours. God looks on us so that we must look differently at ourselves and at others.

—Michael J. Glodo, *The Lord Bless You and Keep You: The Promise of the Gospel in the Aaronic Blessing* (Wheaton: Crossway, 2023), 172.

not orphans. Consequently, because we know our loving, holy, and attentive Father is at hand, we do not reserve our prayers and petitions for special occasions but offer them throughout the day. We offer prayers "with thanksgiving" because we are confident in the character of the One we are addressing. We present our requests not to a nameless void, not to a vague power, but to the Father of our Lord Jesus Christ, who has given us his Spirit. He is *our* God! Whereas we are finite, he is infinite, good, wise, and faithful. So we make our request to him, confident that he is near.

How might our lives change if we just chewed on simple promises like "The Lord is near" as cows chew on their cud? We sometimes make meditating on Scripture too difficult, too sophisticated, too spiritual for those of us who are not super-saints. But meditating is just taking a biblical truth (e.g., "the Lord is near") and savoring it throughout the day—thinking about it, resting in its assurance, allowing the thought to run over us like a purifying stream on a hot summer day. These truths often take a while to penetrate our souls, so we must spend time with and rest in them. Beloved, *the Lord is near*. Only because of this reality can we be thankful even during times that warrant lament.

God's presence, then, provides the "peace of God," which goes beyond our ability to understand how all the pieces fit together (Phil. 4:7). God's peace "will guard your hearts and your minds in Christ Jesus."

Christians are remarkable and different because they are discouraged from picking between an honest assessment of hardships and hopeful confidence in God's presence. After all, Paul penned this instruction while in prison. The joy he writes of is not restricted to the absence of genuine distress and injustice. As New Testament scholar Lynn H. Cohick reminds us, "The source of the Philippians' joy is participation in God's unfolding story of redemption. . . . This joy comes not from achievement but from abiding with God, no matter what."[2] Christians do not have to choose between lament and gratitude because we recognize both that we are vulnerable creatures living in a fallen world and that our God is infinite, wise, good, and present, filled with compassion and care for his people.

QUESTIONS FOR REFLECTION

- Does Paul's directive to "rejoice in the Lord always" sound hopeful or hurtful to you? Why do you think it hits you the way it does?

- How might looking to Christ help us to be brutally honest about our challenges, even as we cultivate lives of joy and praise?

- How might slowly savoring a simple biblical text shape your daily experience? Why do you think we so rarely do this in practice? Consider chewing on the phrase "the Lord is near" for the next few days and see if that helps cultivate an awareness of God's presence and provision.

Remember, Look, and Identify

We are constantly tempted, as Adam was at the beginning, to think that we are actually sufficient unto ourselves, that we have life in ourselves.

—John Behr, *Becoming Human*

Yesterday we considered how Paul calls us to consistently practice gratitude amid the limits of life. Breaking down this practice into three movements helps us incorporate it into our daily routine: remember, look, and identify.

To be a grateful people, we first need to *remember* what God has done in salvation history. From the exodus onward, exercising memory has always been a key practice for God's people. Remember what God has done. Exodus always precedes Sinai; deliverance always comes before and informs commands. We too easily forget this, so we must constantly remind ourselves that Jesus is the Messiah, our Savior, and the risen Lord, who has secured deliverance for us. Never forget. Always remember.

Christians are not merely historians, however, since we also *look* to the present. God continues to be among us and active in and through us. Not only did God work yesterday, but he still works today. He constantly brings salvation and liberating transformation to his people. We look not simply for God's power in the sunrise as we stand in awe before the vast ocean. We also look for signs of hope amid the ashes, for his presence and kindness in unexpected places, not because he delights in pain and suffering but because Christ is our sympathetic high priest, promising to make all things new. Even in the ashes, we proclaim a gospel of hope because Christ is Lord there too: no place is beyond his grasp, his renewal, his redemption.

Further, we do not merely *remember* what God has done and *look* for what he is doing; we also *identify* the works of God that remind us of his character, activity, and presence. To identify these works is to name them as his—he did *that* and *this*, and we will remember all of it and give thanks. When Paul calls us to "continue steadfastly in prayer," he also calls us to be "watchful in it with thanksgiving" (Col. 4:2). If we are not watchful, we will not identify what God is doing, and when that happens, we cease to be a grateful people. When we are ungrateful, our thanksgiving is replaced with grumbling; in our grumbling, we start to imagine that God is distant and cruel rather than present and concerned. We may remember that Daniel prayed three times a day, but during those prayers he also "gave thanks" (Dan. 6:10). He cultivated a disposition of gratitude partly because he realized how little control he had in this world.

There is probably no stronger encouragement to us to persevere than the knowledge that God is persevering with us. We are often tempted to turn in upon ourselves. Then we need to turn out towards God and the many assurances we find in his word that he will never leave us and never forsake us.

—Sinclair B. Ferguson, *The Christian Life: A Doctrinal Introduction*
(Carlisle, PA: Banner of Truth, 1981), 177–78.

Paul calls us to practice thanksgiving by noticing God's fingerprints. He exhorts the beloved: "Whatever is true, whatever is honorable, whatever is just, whatever is pure, whatever is lovely, whatever is commendable, if there is any excellence, if there is anything worthy of praise, think about these things" (Phil. 4:8). Identifying these traits reminds us of the good Creator and Sustainer, who has not abandoned his world to evil and misery but remains present and active.

We push against despair with gratitude and thanksgiving. Finding the fingerprints of God around us requires practice, intent, and perhaps even some training. Those who attend to the path will find plenty of reasons to be grateful and rejoice, but those who stop looking will only grow further disillusioned and distressed.

We rejoice because we remember what God has done, we look for what he is doing, and we identify his presence and kindness in whatever is good, noble, just, peace producing, and worthy of praise. Sometimes we give thanks for the brave young girl who stands up to the bully, for the baker who offers stunningly good sourdough bread. We are grateful to God for friendships, for those who are willing to "[defend] the cause of the poor and needy" (Jer. 22:16 NIV), and for acts of gentleness in a hostile world. We are grateful for a cool glass of water and a kind word, for the warmth of the sun and for a well-built automobile. We don't need to be infinite to recognize God's good presence and provision, and this perception brings us confidence and comfort even amid our finite and fallen lives.

Most of all, we are a grateful people because we are confident of who God is and that God is with us, because we see Christ and are filled with his Spirit. The wickedness, the sadness, and the frustrations all remain worthy of our lamentation and action, but our laments are not all that exists. Christ did not merely die; he also rose and will come again.

QUESTIONS FOR REFLECTION

- Is it easy for you to find comfort and strength when remembering what God has done in the past? Or is it difficult? Why do you think that is?

- Looking around you, what in your life fits the description of Philippians 4:8?

- Psychological research has found that "highly grateful people, as compared to their less grateful counterparts, tend to experience positive emotions more often, enjoy greater satisfaction with life and more hope, and experience less depression, anxiety, and envy. They tend to score higher in pro-sociality and be more empathic, forgiving, helpful, and supportive as well as less focused on materialistic pursuits."[1] If someone keeps a simple gratitude journal for a month, they can measure various physical changes for the better, from lower blood pressure to improved immune systems, from better sleep to increased energy levels. While in some ways these findings should not surprise Christians—and while we don't practice gratitude for the sake of empirical benefits—these conclusions nevertheless make sense given how God has designed the world. Consider writing down five different things each day to thank God for (e.g., a crisp apple, a beautiful view, and gainful employment). After you do this for at least a week, consider how God might use such a simple practice to grow you in grace and truth.

Sleep as a Spiritual Discipline

Since the body is the location in which spirituality is lived out, the richness of our spiritual life depends on how we view life cycles, aging, beauty, intimacy, illness, and finally our own death.
—Lillian Calles Barger, *Eve's Revenge*

We tend to view sleep not as a spiritual matter but only as a physical process: we go through our days, and whenever we are finally done and tired, we go to sleep. Really, there's nothing more to it, is there? Well, maybe there is. When we are deprived of sleep for an extended time, we quickly see just how essential it is to human existence. Not only do we tend to get grumpy and sick, but our hearts also often grow more open to sin, doubts, self-condemnation, and fears.

Although sleep is a blessing, struggling to sleep is not necessarily linked to a moral cause. Problems with sleeping occur for all kinds of reasons at many different ages. The environment, relationships, and even beliefs can all affect the quality of our sleep. Yet whatever the challenges, sleep is part of God's good design for humans.

Sleep reminds us every day that we are creatures, not the Creator. God never sleeps. We usually take that for granted, but we should stop and think about it for a minute. Never. Ever. Sleeps. This gives profound comfort to vulnerable creatures who live in a hostile world. When you are on the front lines, you can't sleep unless someone watches your back. If we don't believe in God, then sleep can terrify us because we imagine that no one is looking out for us. Sleep reminds us that we don't sustain the world. God does. "My help comes from the LORD, who made heaven and earth. He will not let your foot be moved; he who keeps you will not slumber. Behold, he who keeps Israel will neither slumber nor sleep" (Ps. 121:2–4). We can sleep because God doesn't: "In peace I will both lie down and sleep; for you alone, O LORD, make me dwell in safety" (4:8; cf. 46:10–11).

Unlike God, we need sleep, and that is a good gift. Jesus also slept. We know he grew tired and weary from his pilgrimages (John 4:6). Once, he was so exhausted that he slept in a boat tossed about in a violent storm (Matt. 8:24; Mark 4:38). As a man, Jesus couldn't endlessly keep going; he needed sleep! We read that during his struggle in the garden of Gethsemane, Jesus "began to be sorrowful and troubled" (Matt. 26:37). This passage reminds us that feeling so "troubled" and even "sorrowful" that you can't sleep is not necessarily sinful. It can represent a proper response to real difficulties and provide an opportunity for us to be with God in a special way.

Nothing is so insufferable to man as to be completely at rest, without passions, without business, without diversion, without study. He then feels his nothingness, his forlornness, his insufficiency, his dependence, his weakness, his emptiness.

—Blaise Pascal, "Misery of Man without God," in *Blaise Pascal*, ed. Charles W. Eliot, Harvard Classics (New York: Collier & Son, 1910), 51.

My own struggles with sleep have often revealed that I'm either failing to trust in God's faithfulness or tempted to feel that God has left me as an orphan (cf. John 14:18). I start to act as if the weight of the world rests on my shoulders. Concerns about my children, spouse, and church, fears about the future and finances, health and happiness—they all weigh on me. This weight inevitably wakes me up and then keeps me from sleep. I can't sleep because I feel a need to constantly watch my back, prepare, and be ahead of the game. When I feel like an orphan or think I'm ignored by God, sleep becomes elusive.

Wrestling with God at night can be a true spiritual battle. For some of us, it is also a medical struggle as sickness or pain keeps us awake. Again, the psalmist models for us the experience of depending on God in the dark. Despite his desire for sleep, he tells God, "You hold my eyelids open; I am so troubled that I cannot speak" (Ps. 77:4). In "the day of [his] trouble," he seeks God even into the late night (77:2). In the dark of night, he confesses his confusion and his struggle to recognize God's provision (77:7–9). The question for the psalmist and for us is this: *Will our circumstances or God's promise shape us?* Facing an uncertain future, the psalmist reminds himself of what he knows:

> I will remember the deeds of the LORD;
>> yes, I will remember your wonders of old.
> I will ponder all your work,
>> and meditate on your mighty deeds. (77:11–12)

He comforts himself by remembering God's words and actions: God has always been present and working, even if his "footprints" have been unseen (77:19). Even if we haven't noticed him, that doesn't mean he is not there.

Sleep is a spiritual discipline that daily reminds us of our lack of control. Just as a king is not saved simply by the size of his army or a warrior by his strength alone (cf. Ps. 33:16–17), so sleep reminds us daily that we can't rescue ourselves. We are never strong enough, we never know enough, we never can do enough to eliminate our vulnerability. And so *sleep is an act of faith.* It requires us to see our finitude as a good part of God's design for us.

QUESTIONS FOR REFLECTION

- Have you ever observed someone disparage sleep (as if the need for a full night of rest is only for the weak)? How do you think this cultural phenomenon is (mis)shaping us?
- What benefits might there be to imagining sleep as a spiritual discipline? What positive changes might such a redefinition mean for your life?
- What doubts or anxieties currently disrupt your sleep? The next time you wake up in the middle of the night, remember that your God rejoices over you with singing (Zeph. 3:17). This is not intended as a solution for insomnia, but how might recalling God's promises reshape your experience in the dark of night?

Christ and the Sabbath

The Stoics say, "Retire within yourselves; it is there you will
find your rest." And that is not true. Others say, "Go out of
yourselves; seek happiness in amusement." And this is not true.
Illness comes. Happiness is neither without us nor within us. It
is in God, both without us and within us.

—Blaise Pascal, *Pensées*, no. 465

Some people are convinced that Christianity is mostly about
checking off items on a to-do list. One of the most attractive
things about our faith, though, has always been its revelation
that we *don't* have to do certain things. The Sabbath—a coun-
tercultural and radical notion in the Bible, especially when compared to the ancient world—illustrates this very point. One day
a week, you don't have to work. Jews were considered lazy because of it. While those in power could rest when they wanted,
slaves and peasants were often unprotected from demands for
endless labor, a terrible burden still on the materially poor
of our day, who have multiple jobs to make ends meet or are
trapped in literal forms of slavery.

If anyone could legitimately ask for unceasing industry, it would be the Creator of heaven and earth. Yet since the beginning, Yahweh has declared that he and his people would reject that notion. From its foundation in the opening creation narrative (Gen. 2:1–3) to its inclusion in the Ten Commandments (Exod. 20:8–11), the call to rest from regular labor has been a defining characteristic of the creator God and his worshipers. Strong and weak, rich and poor, female and male—all are to be free at least one day in seven, free for unhindered worship, refreshment, and renewal.

Amid the endless demands of life and labor, one day a week has been treated differently, reminding Israel and the church that God, not creatures, upholds the world and calls it good. We were designed not only to work but also to rest, just as God rested after six days of creative work. Yahweh looked back at his creation in delight and satisfaction, declaring the seventh day holy, different, and dedicated to him.

The Sabbath was instituted not to make God's people feel guilty but to make us feel known and loved. It was meant to reorient us and help us experience God and his world. As Jesus later explained, "The Sabbath was made for man, not man for the Sabbath" (Mark 2:27). Contradicting our temptation to think that God's love for us depends on our productivity, one day a week, the Lord says, "Stop; look up; look around; lift your heart; delight and rest." Without this rhythm, we easily stick to our labor and make *it* our lord; we start to worship the creation rather than the Creator. This is why we must rest,

To observe the Sabbath is to celebrate the coronation of a day in the spiritual wonderland of time, the air of which we inhale when we "call it a delight."

—Abraham Joshua Heschel, *The Sabbath*
(New York: Farrar, Straus & Giroux, 1975), 18.

There is perhaps no single thing that could better help us recover Jesus' lordship in our frantic, power-hungry world than to allow him to be Lord of our rest as well as our work. The challenge is disarmingly simple: one day a week, not to do anything that we know to be work.

—Andy Crouch, *Playing God: Redeeming the Gift of Power*
(Downers Grove, IL: IVP Books, 2013), 252.

not because God needs us but because we need him. When we ignore our need to rest, we ignore our limits, and we end up ignoring God himself.

Many who have grown up in legalistic settings, where adherence to the Sabbath is demanded in a crushing and solemn way, experience no joy or delight in this day. But when I encounter Christians who have never really been introduced to the biblical promise of a day of rest, this sounds like one of the most radical and liberating ideas they have ever heard. They just cannot believe it could be possible. "You don't have to work for a whole day?" Such a day sounds genuinely luxurious to them. The God of Scripture is very different from the gods of this age, who regularly reduce us to economic output and endless productivity.

Biblically, though, the Sabbath points beyond mere physical rest to full shalom with God, our neighbors, and the rest of creation. We are given this divinely secured rest, however, only in the Messiah.

The author of Hebrews encourages us not to harden our hearts but to turn again in trust to God (Heb. 3:7–19). To enter into God's rest is to abide in Christ, to be found in him. The Gospels show us that the Creator is also the Redeemer. Jesus, the incarnate Son of God, has done the work of new—and thus renewed—creation. Accordingly, after his life and death, the Messiah rose from the grave and ascended into the heavens. And in his rising we encounter not only the beginning of a new creation but also a fresh invitation to rest. The work of redemption is now completed in Christ, so that "it is finished" (John 19:30). Nothing else needs to be done: your sins are taken away, and you are a new creation.

Our rest is not located and secured simply in creation, but in redemption and the promises yet to be fulfilled. We enter into God's rest, the rest of the same God who entered our world and did what we could not do (Heb. 4:9–11). As John Murray concludes, "The Sabbath is not only a memorial of creation completed and redemption accomplished; it is also the promise of a glorious prospect, the foretaste of the Sabbath rest that remains for the people of God."[1]

Beloved, you and I are secure in the love of the Father, the grace of the Son, and the fellowship of the Spirit. May this security allow us to celebrate our limits as part of God's good work. May this security drive us back to our God, to one another, and even to our right dependence on the rest of creation. May this security encourage our work, liberate our rest, and free us to love and serve others. God has made us to be limited creatures, able to participate freely in his work, confident in his presence, and grateful for his promises and provision. Let us appreciate the goodness of our finitude as we rest in the love and provision of our infinitely good God. May it be so.

QUESTIONS FOR REFLECTION

- Have you seen or participated in debates about the Sabbath? Understanding this day not as a legalistic requirement but as an invitation by our good Creator, how might engaging in the weekly practice of rest change your life?

- Do you feel guilty or lazy when you devote a whole day to corporate worship, shared meals, and physical rest and refreshment? If so, why do you think that is? If not, what helps you maintain your perspective?

- Recall Jesus's words in Mark 2:27: "The Sabbath was made for man, not man for the Sabbath." What does this verse mean in its context?

- The idea of not doing homework can sound crazy to high school and college students. Not studying on Sunday might even make them feel guilty; when asked, many admit they suspect that God is disappointed with them—or at least their parents are! But what if the moral shortcoming isn't that they take a day off from their regular work? What if their shortcoming is that they imagine they can and should work constantly? What if we believed that what's offensive to God isn't that we stop working before dinner or don't do regular work on Sunday—but that we think we should *always* be working? Or maybe God is less offended and just raises an eyebrow at our naivete. Consider discussing these matters with other Christians, avoiding anger or getting defensive while also seeking an honest discussion.

- Our Sabbath rest is ultimately in Christ. How might you cultivate a rest in Christ's finished work on the cross and in his ongoing heavenly ministry on your behalf? How might such a perspective change the ways you speak and act?

Acknowledgments

This book came to fruition only because of the encouragement, help, and prayers of others; so as briefly as I can, I would like to express my deepest gratitude to some key people. Charity Chaney, my work-study student, helped provide initial suggestions for many of the forty entries, creating a framework I could build on. Your diligence and kindness in that work were such a help to me. After I crafted the material, I tapped many gracious friends to serve as initial editors and test readers, each providing valuable feedback and encouragement. While I would prefer writing paragraphs about each of these people, to keep these acknowledgments manageable, I'll restrict myself to simply mentioning key names: John Yates, Aly Davis, Eric and Jodi Blick, Mattie Livingston, Elizabeth Messer, and Christy Grauley. You each know how much time and guidance you provided. Because you all brought different instincts, backgrounds, and skills, the result was a rich array of feedback and timely encouragement. While any shortcomings of this book are ultimately my responsibility, so much of the good that I hope comes through these pages can be traced to the gifts these friends gave along the way. Thank you!

As always, I am thankful to Tabitha. Recently celebrating our thirty-first anniversary, I have felt afresh the great kindness of God that I received when you married me. Thank you for consistently telling me "It's enough" and for pointing me to God's delight and sufficiency. Yours is the voice I trust most, and I cannot imagine navigating this life without you. Jonathan, my son, you have been so faithful in praying for me, providing laughter and thoughtful words of grace, and helping me believe this work matters and can be genuinely helpful to people. I dedicated *You're Only Human* to you because of the many ways you center and ground my life, helping me reimagine what faithfulness looks like for God's children. All of that remains true. I love you, buddy.

Finally, I dedicate this book to my daughter Margot. I don't believe this project would have moved forward without you. Never will I forget sitting at the airport and talking to you about the crazy idea of this devotional, and you jumped at it. You promised to help (and you did), and you made me believe that it would be possible, even amid the other pressing demands in my life. It was you, along with Charity, who first helped me decide on material for the entries. It was you who would tell me over lunch, "You got this, no worries." To get pep talks from your kids is a strange and beautiful gift, and you are one of the best in the world to give them! I smile just thinking about it. So I joyfully dedicate this devotional to you, grateful to God for your unique combination of a brilliant intellect, authentic humility, relational wisdom, and a service-oriented life. Those who know you will testify that I didn't just describe a romanticized ideal of my daughter; I described a genuine, godly woman named Margot. I will never tire of seeing your smile and your zeal for life. I love you so much.

Notes

Day 2

1. Gerhard von Rad, *Old Testament Theology*, vol. 1, *The Theology of Israel's Historical Traditions*, trans. D. M. G. Stalker (New York: Harper & Row, 1962), 160.

Day 6

1. Constantine R. Campbell, *Paul and Union with Christ: An Exegetical and Theological Study* (Grand Rapids: Zondervan, 2012), 414.

2. John Calvin, *Institutes of the Christian Religion*, ed. John T. McNeill, trans. Ford Lewis Battles (Philadelphia: Westminster, 1960), 3.1.1 (p. 537).

Day 7

1. Lilian Calles Barger, *Eve's Revenge: Women and a Spirituality of the Body* (Grand Rapids: Brazos, 2003), 101.

Day 8

1. Payam Ebizadeh, "Fifty Is the New Thirty: See the Reasons Why," *Splash Magazines*, July 18, 2018, https://splashmags.com/index.php/2018/07/12/fifty-is-the-new-thirty-see-the-reason-why.

Day 11

1. Tertullian, *On Prayer* 18, in *The Ante-Nicene Fathers: Translations of the Writings of the Fathers down to A.D. 325*, ed. Alexander Roberts and James Donaldson, 10 vols. (Peabody, MA: Hendrickson, 1994), 3:686–87.

2. Daniel B. Hinshaw, *Touch and the Healing of the World* (New York: St. Vladimir's Seminary Press, 2017), 118.

3. Rodney Stark, *The Rise of Christianity* (Princeton: Princeton University Press, 1996), esp. chap. 5; and Mike Aquilina and James L. Papandrea,

How Christianity Saved Civilization (New York: Image Books, 2015; repr., Manchester: Sophia Institute, 2018), esp. chap. 3.

Day 12

1. Bessel van der Kolk, *The Body Keeps the Score: Brain, Mind, and Body in the Healing of Trauma* (New York: Penguin, 2015), 217.

Day 13

1. Stanley Hauerwas and William H. Willimon, *The Truth about God: The Ten Commandments in Christian Life* (Nashville: Abingdon, 1999), 68.

Day 15

1. Dietrich Bonhoeffer, sermon on Luke 17:33, Madrid, Spain, October 21, 1928, in *Barcelona, Berlin, New York, 1928–1931*, ed. Clifford J. Green, trans. Douglas W. Stott, Dietrich Bonhoeffer Works 10 (Minneapolis: Fortress, 2008), 532–35. All quotes in this entry come from this source.

Day 17

1. Susan Eastman, "Double Participation and the Responsible Self in Romans 5–8," in *Apocalyptic Paul: Cosmos and Anthropos in Romans 5–8*, ed. Beverly Gaventa (Waco: Baylor University Press, 2013), 107.

Day 18

1. Alasdair MacIntyre, *After Virtue*, 3rd ed. (Notre Dame, IN: University of Notre Dame Press, 2007), 184.

Day 19

1. Bernard of Clairvaux, *The Twelve Degrees of Humility and Pride*, part 1, chap. 1, trans. Barton R. V. Mills (CreateSpace, 2010), 11 (emphasis added).

2. This story and the responses come from *The Desert Fathers: Sayings of the Early Christian Monks*, trans. Benedicta Ward (London: Penguin, 2003), 154 ("Humility," no. 19).

Day 20

1. Thomas Aquinas, *Summa Theologica*, trans. Fathers of the English Dominican Province (New York: Benziger Brothers, 1948), II-II, q. 161, art. 1 (p. 1842).

2. Aquinas, *Summa Theologica*, II-II, q. 161, art. 2, reply to obj. 2 (p. 1843). He later adds, "Excessive self-confidence is more opposed to humility than lack of confidence is," q. 161, art. 2, reply to obj. 3 (p. 1843).

3. G. K. Chesterton, *Saint Thomas Aquinas: "The Dumb Ox"* (Garden City, NY: Image Books, 1956), 90. I am here drawing these quotes from Mary M. Keys's wonderfully stimulating essay, "Statesmanship, Humility, and Happiness: Reflections on Robert Faulkner's The Case for Greatness," in *Perspectives on Political Science* 39, no. 4 (October–December 2010): 194.

4. Mary Keys—one of the most able interpreters of Aquinas on this— nicely captures this twofold dynamic: "Magnanimity aids a person in daring good and great deeds according to true dictates of reason and despite formidable dangers and difficulties; humility keeps this passion for greatness from feeding the flame of hubris and motivating irrational, vicious action under the cloak of what seems honorable and outstanding" ("Statesmanship, Humility, and Happiness," 195).

5. Aquinas, *Summa Theologica*, II-II, q. 133, art. 1, reply to obj. 3 (p. 1737).

Day 22

1. Augustine, *Confessions* 11.14, trans. Henry Chadwick (Oxford: Oxford University Press, 1991), 230.

2. Judy Wajcman, *Pressed for Time: The Acceleration of Life in Digital Capitalism* (Chicago: University of Chicago Press, 2015), 31.

3. John O'Donohue, *To Bless the Space between Us: A Book of Blessings* (New York: Doubleday, 2008), immediately preceding the poem "To the Exhausted."

Day 24

1. Alexander Schmemann, *For the Life of the World: Sacraments and Orthodoxy* (New York: St. Vladimir's Seminary Press, 2018), 140.

2. Schmemann, *For the Life of the World*, 143.

Day 25

1. Peter Lombard, *The Sentences, Book 3: On the Incarnation of the Word*, trans. Guilio Silano, Mediaeval Sources in Translation 45 (Toronto: Pontifical Institute of Mediaeval Studies, 2008), 34.3 (p. 138) (emphasis added).

Day 27

1. "Indulgent," Myefe.com, accessed September 30, 2024, https://myefe .com/transcription-pronunciation/indulgent.

Day 28

1. See, e.g., the helpful discussion of *anakephalaiōsis* (recapitulation) in Robert M. Grant, *Irenaeus of Lyons*, Early Church Fathers (London: Routledge, 1997), 50–53.

Day 32

1. Gerald L. Sittser, *Water from a Deep Well: Christian Spirituality from Early Martyrs to Modern Missionaries* (Downers Grove, IL: IVP Books, 2007), 264–68.

Day 33

1. Irwyn L. Ince Jr., *The Beautiful Community: Unity, Diversity, and the Church at Its Best* (Downers Grove, IL: InterVarsity, 2020).

2. John Baillie, *A Diary of Private Prayer* (New York: Charles Scribner's Sons, 1955), 81, day 19 (emphasis added).

Day 35

1. Jocelyn K. Glei, "Productivity Shame," *HurrySlowly*, podcast, May 14, 2019, https://hurryslowly.co/216-jocelyn-k-glei.

Day 36

1. Brené Brown, "The Power of Vulnerability," TED, June 2010, https://www.ted.com/talks/brene_brown_the_power_of_vulnerability.

2. Curt Thompson, *The Soul of Shame: Retelling the Stories We Believe about Ourselves* (Downers Grove, IL: IVP Books, 2015), 120.

Day 37

1. Gordon Fee, *Philippians*, IVP New Testament Commentary Series (Downers Grove, IL: InterVarsity, 1999), 407.

2. Lynn H. Cohick, *Philippians*, ed. Tremper Longman III and Scott Mc-Knight, Story of God Commentary 11 (Grand Rapids: Zondervan, 2013), 219.

Day 38

1. Giacomo Bono, Mikki Krakauer, and Jeffrey J. Froh, "The Power and Practice of Gratitude," in *Positive Psychology in Practice: Promoting Human Flourishing in Work, Health, Education, and Everyday Life*, ed. Stephen Joseph (Hoboken, NJ: John Wiley & Sons, 2015), 561.

Day 40

1. John Murray, "The Sabbath Institution," in *Collected Writings* (Edinburgh: Banner of Truth, 1976), 1:216. See also his brief essay in the same volume: "The Pattern of the Lord's Day," 219–24.